AMERICA'S
STEALTH
FIGHTERS AND BOMBERS

James C. Goodall

Motorbooks International
Publishers & Wholesalers ®

James Warren Goodall,
the best son a dad could ever have. I'm proud to be your dad.

First published in 1992 by Motorbooks International Publishers & Wholesalers, PO Box 2, 729 Prospect Avenue, Osceola, WI 54020 USA

Motorbooks International books are also available at discounts in bulk quantity for industrial or sales-promotional use. For details write to Special Sales Manager at the Publisher's address

Library of Congress Cataloging-in-Publication Data
Goodall, James C.
    America's stealth fighters and bombers / James. C. Goodall.
      p. cm.
    Includes index.
    ISBN 0-87938-609-6
    1. Stealth aircraft—United States. I. Title.
UG1242.S73G66   1992
358.4'283—dc20   92-10964

Printed and bound in Hong Kong

On the front cover: *The Lockheed Skunk Works has upheld their reputation for innovative and successful design with the F-117A Stealth Fighter and YF-22 Advanced Tactical Fighter.* Lockheed

On the frontispiece: *An F-117A wings its way to Saudi Arabia.* Mike Dornheim *Aviation Week & Space Technology*

On the title page: *Lockheed's YF-22 Advanced Tactical Fighters.* Lockheed

On the back cover: *Upper left, the Northrop YF-23 showing all its control surfaces deflected.* Northrop. *Upper right, the state-of-the-art cockpit of the Northrop B-2 Stealth Bomber.* Northrop. *Lower left, this time-lapsed photo shows thrust vectoring in action on the YF-119-PW engine used in one of the YF-22 prototypes.* Pratt & Whitney via Arnie Gunderson

Contents

Acknowledgments

I would like to use this space to thank a whole lot of people, and in the process I'll probably leave out a few. First and foremost I must thank Bill Sweetman who got me going in our first effort, *Lockheed F-117A Stealth Fighter*, and to Mary Pat Sweetman, maker of the best chocolate chip cookies anywhere. Steve Paulson, an F-117A pilot who went out on a limb and allowed me to interview him months before anyone knew anything about the F-117A. Mr. Pete Eames, Program Security for Special Projects in the Pentagon, located in room 5D156. My best friend, John Andrews of the Testor Corporation, who I call *Spy One*: I didn't think it would ever be this much fun when we first met in the summer of 1975. M. Sgt. Bobby Sheldon, Public Affairs NCO for the 37th Tactical Fighter Wing, now the 49th Fighter Wing: I know your hands were tied in responding to most of my requests, but thanks for the ones you did respond to. The two commanders of the 37th Tactical Fighter Wing that I met from a distance, Col. Tony Tolin and Col. Al Whitley: you and your team of Stealth drivers did one hell of a job over the skies of Baghdad. Mr. Ben R. Rich and the entire team of Black Jet builders and designers: Thanks for the fun of seeing it all come together. Bill Park, the first man to fly Have Blue among other Lockheed planes. Richard Stadler, chief of public relations for the Lockheed Advanced Development Company. The best photographers that Lockheed could have, Denny Lombard and Eric Schulzinger. Mike Dornheim of *Aviation Week and Space Technology*. Col. Ken Dyson, US Air Force retired. A very special thanks goes out to the man who tried to fly the very first F-117A, and nearly lost his life in the process, Robert L. Riedenauer, who his friends call "R plus nine": I hope I got your name spelled right this time. To a number of former Lockheed Advanced Development Company employees that I can't mention, not because they violated security—they didn't—but just because. To the entire Public Affairs staff of the 57th Fighter Wing at Nellis Air Force Base, Nevada. Colonel Sconyer, Lt. Col. Weber, and Capt. Kevin Baggett, Tactical Air Command Headquarters Public Affairs. Maj. Greg Kreiss, 57th Fighter Wing Public Affairs; you put on one great Stealth show. Fellow photographer and good friend Tony Landis; in the four years we have been shooting airplanes together, we have never photographed a normal aircraft. To all the photographers who have helped me over the years, including Chuck Mayer, Dave Prettyman, Randy Kovisko, Terry Love, Sid Bremer, Chris Mayer, Dave Brown, Jerry Geer, Doug Slowiak, Kevin Patrick, Brian C. Rogers, Mick Roth, Don McGarry, Mike Quan, and Mike Groove. Knox Bishop and Dick Cole, two of the best the International Plastic Modeler's Society has to offer. Jay Miller, the hardest working man I know; if I worked one-tenth as hard as he does, I could become one of the best authors in the field, behind of course Bill Sweetman and Jay Miller. A special thanks to Tim Parker, the publisher of Motorbooks International, and Greg Field, aerospace editor, for all their patience over the last twelve trying months. I thank you all.

This entire process began over twelve years ago because a very well known author, Jeff Ethell, gave me a push to do something on the SR-71; well Jeff, I'm on my way. On October 28, 1991, a New York Air National Guard C-5A, flown by the members of the 137th Military Airlift Squadron, transported to Minneapolis, Minnesota, the eighth production Lockheed A-12. It now takes its place of honor as the centerpiece of the Minnesota Air Guard Museum.

Jim Goodall

The Northrop B-2A Stealth Bomber. Northrop

7

Introduction

Stealth, the Edge for the Twenty-first Century

"Stealth gives us back that fundamental element of war called surprise," John J. Welch, Jr., assistant secretary of the Air Force for acquisition, said shortly after the end of Operation Desert Storm. "Anytime you're able to keep surprise, you keep the advantage."

That edge or upper hand that Secretary Welch refers to was spectacularly demonstrated night after night over the skies of Baghdad, Iraq, by the Air Force Lockheed F-117A Stealth Fighters during the six weeks of Desert Storm. The Black Jet flew into the heart of the world's most heavily defended air space and came back unscathed. The air over Baghdad was tougher, in fact, than North Atlantic Treaty Organization (NATO) forces would have encountered if they would have gone against in Eastern European forces and targets, said Secretary of the Air Force Donald B. Rice.

"We've seen that not only does stealth work, but that it puts fewer assets at risk and saves lives," Rice said at a briefing during Stealth Week activities in mid-June 1991.

During the 1991 Gulf War, F-117As represented only two percent of the attack aircraft in the theater but took out over forty percent of the strategic targets. The force of forty-three F-117As that

operated during the air campaign of Desert Storm suffered no losses, even though it went against one of the most modern and highly integrated air defense systems in the world.

The advantage of stealth technology can best be demonstrated during the air raids on the nuclear reactor facility south of Baghdad. A strike force of conventional aircraft made up of sixty attack, fighter, Wild Weasel (surface-to-air missile [SAM] destroyer), and electronic countermeasures (ECM) aircraft, plus fifteen KC-135 aerial tankers, failed in their efforts to destroy the reactor facility.

Call in the F-117A Stealth Fighter. With the support of only two aerial tankers, versus fifteen for the unsuccessful raid, eight F-117A aircraft, versus sixty conventional aircraft, eight F-117As carrying sixteen laser-guided bombs destroyed three of the four reactors in one raid. Fewer planes and, more importantly, fewer lives were put at risk because of stealth.

"Stealth saves lives, money, and does the job better," Rice said. "It sounds like the kind of thing we need in the force," he added, advocating the need for the B-2 Stealth Bomber and the F-22A Advanced Tactical Fighter.

With the F-117A and Advanced Cruise Missile already fielded, adding the B-2A and F-22A will give the Air Force the right mix of stealth and conventional technology to tackle mission

requirements well into the twenty-first century.

Stealth does not spell an end to conventional forces, said Rice. "Stealth aircraft will complement, not replace nonstealthy aircraft in the current inventory. We will still have F-16s and F-15Es and other nonstealthy aircraft in the force structure for a long time to come," the secretary added. "But we need that cutting edge component of the force that can go in the lead on day one against the toughest defenses."

"Everyone now agrees the F-117 was a real bargain," Rice said. "I visited with F-117 pilots who came back from the war and asked them what would they do to improve their machines. And their answers were more range and payload. Sounds like the B-2 to me. The B-2 will give us five to six times the unrefueled range, will carry up to ten times the payload of the F-117, but cost five to six times as much. Any way you slice it, we're getting a lot more delivery payload per dollar expended from the B-2 than we get out of the F-117."

Stealth costs more, initially. The B-2 bomber's flyaway cost is $437.4 million in fiscal 1991 dollars. But comparing total costs for the B-52 and B-47, the B-2 actually costs less. "We have to keep affordability in context," said Secretary Welch. "What things do you buy today that don't cost two, three, even seven times as much as they did in the 1950s [when the Air Force purchased the B-52

Northrop's two Stealth designs, the YF-23 Advanced Tactical Fighter and the B-2A Advanced Technology Bomber. Northrop

and B-47]?" He pointed out that we spend a smaller percentage of our military budget on the B-2 than we did on the B-52 and B-47. When you add into the equation all the dollars spent over the last thirty-five years to keep the B-52 current, the B-2's cost seems even more reasonable.

A recent Air Force Association paper on the B-2 put the value into proper context. "The B-2 has a greater range than the B-1B and B-52H when flying comparable mission profiles with the same or larger payload. Stationed in just three bases, one in the continental United States and two overseas (Diego Garcia in the Indian Ocean and Guam in the Pacific), B-2s could hit targets virtually anywhere in the world in a matter of

hours with just one refueling, minimal preparation time, and few support assets. No other weapon system can."

With the B-2, the United States gets a multirole weapon that can perform conventional, strategic, and even maritime missions if purchased in sufficient numbers.

Aviation Week & Space Technology for the week of January 20, 1992, reported that the House of Representatives has already voted to keep the B-2 production at fifteen airplanes, and said that ten operational B-2s are sufficient to conduct military operations.

But Air Force Secretary Rice said ten B-2s are not enough. "The latest independent studies show that kind of conventional operations, which would call strongly for the use of the capabilities that the B-2 offers, demand operational forces in the range of forty, fifty, or sixty bombers, depending on what range of scenarios you're handling,"

Next page
The Lockheed YF-22 Advanced Tactical Fighter. Lockheed

Rice told the Senate Armed Services Committee on 19 June 1991.

In making a case for the F-22A, Secretary Welch said, "With the F-22, we can ensure air superiority, an element we've controlled since World War II. Once you get air superiority, you can do all the other things. Without it, you can't do very much."

The same feeling was voiced by Gen. John Michael Loh, commander of Tactical Air Command, in testimony to Congress. "We need the F-22 for three reasons," he said. "First, air superiority is our most critical mission because it gives all our forces the freedom of action and ability to conduct all other air and ground missions.

Lockheed F-117A Stealth Fighters after returning from Operation Desert Storm. James C. Goodall

"Second, the former Soviets [now called the Commonwealth of Independent States] continue to modernize all elements of their air defense system and are willing to export them virtually around the world (this is our greatest threat now that the Soviet Union no longer exists). We need the ability to penetrate, operate in, survive, and destroy targets in the sophisticated air defense environment of the future for all regional contingencies.

"Finally, it is impossible to give the aging F-15 the combination of stealth,

supersonic cruise, supportability, and the weapons we get with the F-22—a combination we must have to maintain our advantage in the air."

The F-22 will be the first aircraft to combine low-observable technology (stealth) and air superiority capabilities. With its superior radar system and weapons such as the Advanced Medium Range Air-to-Air Missile (AMRAAM), it will have first-look, first-shoot, and first-kill capabilities.

The arguments against the F-22 include its cost (just under $60 billion for approximately 650 aircraft) and the fact that the Air Force currently enjoys air superiority with the F-15 that saw its first flight over twenty years ago with its roots going back to the Robert S. McNamara

generated requirements of the early to mid-1960s. (McNamara was secretary of defense during the John Kennedy and Lyndon Johnson administrations.) By the time the first operational F-22A goes into squadron service in the mid- to late 1990s, the basic F-15 design will be over thirty-five years old.

Advanced aircraft such as the Russian MiG-29, MiG-31, Su-27, and France's Mirage family of aircraft are in the hands of many third world countries. These same aircraft have already been called aerodynamic equals to the F-15. Secretary Rice said the real issue is "air superiority into the next century. We're not interested in an even match in the skies. We're interested in maintaining American air superiority."

The Lockheed F-117A Stealth Fighter.
Lockheed

Lockheed's two Stealth designs, the F-117A
and YF-22. Lockheed

Stealth Design

"Some have said that stealth technology is perhaps the most revolutionary set of military technologies since the advent of radar and the atomic bomb."
—*A Pentagon Spokesman*

When someone talks of stealth the first thing that comes to mind is the Lockheed Black Jet, the F-117A Stealth Fighter. But stealth isn't the product of the Lockheed Skunk Works (officially the Advanced Development Company), or of Northrop for that matter. It isn't something that you can put your hand or finger on. Stealth isn't an object or a thing. It is a process that involves a host of technologies that when combined actively or passively reduces the various signatures of an aircraft, missile, ship, or any other detectable object.

Stealth isn't just the reduction of the radar signature that is referred to so often. The physical shape or material of an aircraft can significantly reduce the radar cross section, but if you don't address the balance of the issues at hand, a smaller radar cross system won't make a bit of difference.

If looks could kill. Aren't you glad you're not looking over your shoulder in a MiG-29 or Su-27? You didn't even know this guy was in your neighborhood until he showed up on your six. Lockheed

Take for example the Lockheed F-117A. The mission profile is to fly the Black Jet only at night. Why? Because the F-117A is such a large visible target the only way to eliminate the visible signature was to paint it black and fly it only at night.

"Stealth is a convenient term adopted for the technology," said Lt. Col. Bud Baker, a member of the B-2A Program Office at Wright-Patterson Air Force Base, Ohio. "Around here, we use the term low observable." Baker works in the US Air Force Aeronautical Systems Division, which manages the F-117A, B-2A, F-22A, and the Advanced Cruise Missile (ACM).

"The first thing people need to realize about low-observable aircraft is that they are not invisible," Baker said.

The total success of the F-117A over the skies of Baghdad has many people thinking that low-observable aircraft are impossible to detect or track. The fact of the matter is that low-observables just make the aircraft much harder to find and even harder to lock onto with radar- or infrared-guided weapons. If you were to direct enough radar energy at a Daisy BB you would get a reflection of enough energy to detect that object.

The advantage, however, is even if ground-based radars could find and lock onto the F-117A, most weapons would not be able to track the F-117A or lock on.

"The whole idea of low-observables is to balance the detectable signatures," said Baker. "It doesn't make sense to minimize the radar signature if the IR or infrared signature is not correspondingly reduced."

Reducing detectability is not a feature exclusive to the Air Force. The Navy has been using stealth features on its nuclear attack and missile submarines for almost thirty years. That is why we are so far ahead of the former Soviet navy in antisubmarine warfare. We can still hear theirs, but they cannot hear or find ours! In the same vein, the Army uses low-observables in reducing infrared signatures of tanks and other vehicles. They have gone so far as to issue infrared low-observable fatigues to all members of the armed services—the current issue battle dress uniforms, or BDUs.

The introduction of low-observables into the Air Force is not something that has just happened in the 1980s and 1990s. Low-observable technology was a primary concern of the forerunner to the Lockheed SR-71, the CIA's single-place Blackbird called the A-12. As early as 1962, Lockheed was actively working on the first truly operational low-observable aircraft, the A-12. By the time the A-12 entered operational service in the mid-1960s, the aircraft's radar cross section had been reduced to a mere twenty-two square inches. Its big brother, the SR-71, featured true first-generation low-observable technology in the form of special coatings and materials. The B-1B

This Lockheed A-12 on the ramp at the Groom Lake test facility is parked in front of the hangars that housed the early Have Blue and YF-117As. The A-12 is a first-generation stealth aircraft. The radar cross section for the A-12 is less than twenty-two square inches. Considering the aircraft is as big as a Boeing 727-100, its cross section is very small indeed. James C. Goodall collection

The canceled B-1A's radar cross section is just over ten square meters. When the B-1 program was revived, the B-1A's dorsal spine was removed to lower the radar cross section. In addition, Rockwell removed the variable inlet ramps, baffeled the inlet path, and applied other low-observable techniques to lower the overall radar cross section of the B-1B by a factor of ten, down to approximately one square meter. James C. Goodall

and the SR-71 are considered to be first-generation stealth aircraft.

Breakthroughs in computer software and hardware in the early 1970s helped to advance stealth technology. A computer program called ECHO enabled Lockheed to accurately predict an aircraft's radar signature and to evaluate new design concepts without actually building and flying the real thing. This technology led to the building of a second-generation low-observable, the Have Blue, a toddler version of the production F-117A Senior Trend aircraft.

In 1975, Lockheed built a large-scale model of Have Blue and transported it to a remote radar test range near Holloman Air Force Base, New Mexico. Both Lockheed and Northrop had designs represented at a radar fly-off with the Lockheed design winning out. The contract was issued to Lockheed in 1976 under the Carter administration, with the first flight of the Have Blue in the winter of 1977. The overall success of the Have Blue design led the Air Force to issue a production contract for the first batch of twenty-four F-117As, with the first full-scale development YF-117 scheduled to fly in July 1980, but delayed until June 1981.

Despite the well publicized success of the F-117A in the Gulf War, the Air Force wants no more than the fifty-six aircraft it has in the inventory. Air Force officials claim the F-117A technology is outdated.

Gen. John Michael Loh, commander of Tactical Air Command, said, "The F-117A is far from the final word on stealth."

Instead of reducing the radar cross section on future designs, the Air Force is emphasizing speed, agility, and state-of-the-art avionics in its next generation fighter. The result is the Lockheed-General Dynamics-Boeing F-22A Advanced Tactical Fighter, a fifth-generation stealth design.

In the 1990s and well into the twenty-first century, radar will remain the principal challenge to low observability. As sensors become more and more capable, additional advances in low observability in the infrared, visual, acoustic, laser, and electromagnetic signatures will challenge military aircraft designers.

Shape is an all-important aspect in producing a smaller radar cross section. The B-2's flying wing shape (and its predecessor's, the Northrop YB-49 of the 1950s) is naturally stealthy. Its smooth seamless contours and its lack of vertical tail assemblies or other protruding edges or shapes represent a smaller target to incoming enemy radar.

"Most of the efforts to reduce the plane's radar cross section go into deflection, absorption, and reflection, in that order," said Lt. Col. Baker. Other technologies used to reduce the radar cross section of aircraft include the use of material that absorbs and deflects the radar waves.

An example of just how well radar-absorbent materials work in the reduction of radar cross section in a particular design, we have to go no further than the B-1A versus the B-1B. The number three B-1A, with its unshrouded inlets and equipment housing, has a radar cross section of approximately ten square meters. The B-1B, with a newly designed ducted inlet, fixed inlet ramp, and a removed spine fairing, was able to reduce its detectable radar signature to one square meter. The

B-2A's radar cross section is about one-hundredth of a square meter.

To reduce the large infrared signature so common in today's jet powered aircraft—and a dead giveaway for modern infrared detection equipment and weapons—stealth aircraft use several different design innovations. Beavertail assemblies (as found on the Lockheed F-117A, baffled engine exhaust outlets found on the F-22 and F-23 Advanced Tactical Fighter candidates, as well as the B-2A Stealth Bomber) help hide the hot exhaust, the major contributor to the infrared signature.

From a purely visual point of view, the F-117A can be seen over thirty miles away in the clear desert sky. The color of the F-117A that makes it so visible in the daytime renders it all but impossible to see at night.

The F-117A blended so well into the night that during preflight and postflight inspections, the ground crew had to feel its way around the airplane in order to avoid its sharp corners and edges.

Stealth technology is a significant challenge for potential adversaries. "Stealth isn't just one technology. It's a host of technologies that are tough to defeat," Lt. Col. Baker said.

Stealth aircraft are neither invisible nor immune to radar or other threats, but pose so many challenges to air defense systems that their survivability is greatly improved over nonstealthy aircraft.

"Ever since the first guy picked up a rock and went after his neighbor, we've had systems and counter systems," Baker said. "Is low-observable technology the end of the step-counter-step? Not likely.

"As long as we've had the vehicles we've tried to make them less vulnerable," he added. "Stealth is just another step in the process."

The Lockheed F-117A Stealth Fighter

During the mid-1970s, Lockheed Skunk Works engineers began working on a computerized program that would allow reduced radar cross section techniques to be coupled with aerodynamics to come up with a flyable aircraft design. One of the successes of the computer program Lockheed developed was the use of faceting, a design process by which the aircraft surface reflects 99.99 percent of the reflected radar energy from the radar source away from its receiver. If such a design could be made to fly, they would have a true stealth aircraft.

Have Blue

Late in 1976, the Skunk Works received a contract from the Defense Advanced Research Projects Agency to build and test two subscale (about sixty percent of actual size) Stealth Strike Fighters, using faceting, under the code name Have Blue.

The Skunk Works built the Have Blue technology demonstrators and shipped them out of the Lockheed Burbank production facility in just a matter of months. The technology demonstrators were built using a large number of off-the-shelf parts to keep production cost down.

A beautiful bird's-eye view of F-117A number 807 taken on the center taxiway at its Tonopah Test Range base. Lockheed

The jet engines were out of a Northrop T-38A Talon. The fly-by-wire components were from the General Dynamics F-16. The landing gear was from the Fairchild/Republic A-10A Thunderbolt II. And the environmental systems were taken from the Lockheed C-130 Hercules.

By using off-the-shelf components, Lockheed built two technology demonstrators in record time and under budget (a trademark of the Skunk Works) for the unheard of sum of only $35 million dollars for both aircraft. The two Have Blue aircraft were disassembled and shipped to the Groom Lake test facility in the Nevada desert for reassembly and flight testing. A strike of Lockheed production personnel forced the management and supervisory team to reassemble the two prototypes.

Chief Lockheed test pilot Bill Park made the first flight of the Have Blue aircraft in late December 1977 or early January 1978 from the Groom Lake test facility.

On 4 May 1978, Park was landing the number one technology demonstrator when a high-sink-rate problem arose. The aircraft hit the ground hard, jamming the right main landing gear in a semiretracted position. Park tried repeatedly to dislodge the jammed gear, but met with no success. He came down hard on the left main gear three times in hopes of dislodging the right gear, even shaking the aircraft trying to unstick the

gear. Nothing seemed to work and Park was told to climb to 10,000 feet, burn off all excess fuel, and eject. The force of the ejection caused his head to hit the head rest, rendering him unconscious when he hit the ground.

Park survived the ejection, but because of the extensive injuries suffered, he was removed from flying status, never to fly again.

From mid-1978 to the loss of the second Have Blue technology demonstrator in early 1980, US Air Force test pilot Lt. Col. Ken Dyson flew the balance of the flight test on the Have Blue program. Dyson flew more than sixty-five sorties, many of them against threat radars on the Nellis Range. These tests played an important part in reducing the radar cross section of the prototype and identifying the need for proper maintenance and preflight inspection of low-observable aircraft.

The shape of the Have Blue was highly classified until the summer of 1990 when two poor quality photos appeared in *Aviation Week and Space Technology*. The shape was ideal for the purposes of reducing the radar cross section to an absolute minimum, but needed to be modified to improve aerodynamic and handling properties and incorporate stealthy sensor stations.

The twin inward-canted rudders were less than effective in controlling pitch and yaw. The primary reason for mounting the rudders in that

HAVE BLUE

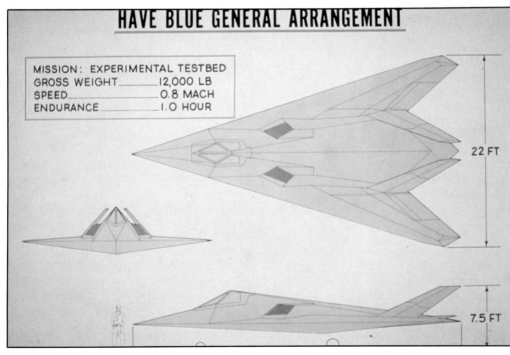

HAVE BLUE GENERAL ARRANGEMENT

MISSION: EXPERIMENTAL TESTBED
GROSS WEIGHT_____12,000 LB
SPEED_____0.8 MACH
ENDURANCE_____1.0 HOUR

22 FT

7.5 FT

The only photo of the Lockheed Have Blue technology demonstrator aircraft released as of this book's press date. Have Blue was a small vehicle measuring only 7.5 feet in height, twenty-two feet in width, and thirty-seven feet in length. Grossing out at a mere 12,000 pounds, Have Blue could fly for only an hour at a time. It did not have air-refueling capabilities and carried no weapons. The photo shown here was taken early in its flight testing and shows the number one test aircraft. By early to mid January 1978, the aircraft had been painted black. The inset is a rear-quarter shot showing the twin inward canted tails. USAF via Tony Landis

A general arrangement drawing of the Have Blue technology demonstrator. USAF via Tony Landis

configuration was to reduce the exhaust of the aircraft's infrared signature, when in fact it acted as an infrared reflector, thus increasing the signature from both the look-down-shoot-down view and ground-based view.

The overall test results of the Have Blue program led William Perry, under secretary of the Air Force for research and engineering, to urge the Air Force to apply stealth technology on an operational airplane. During the final months of the Carter Administration, Secretary of Defense Harold Brown made the announcement that the

A view of the Groom Lake test facility taken on 4 February 1992. Since the last published photo of this facility (taken in September 1978 by John Lear and seen only in Lockheed F-117A—Operation and Development of the Stealth Fighter by Bill Sweetman and James C. Goodall), the compound has more than doubled in size. Groom Lake was observed for over six hours on 4 February 1992 and all that was seen was a B-2A flying overhead and six Boeing 737s owned by EG&G come and go, transporting the company's technicians, but it was still a sight to behold. Behind what used to be the Lockheed A-12 hangars is a production complex similar in size and shape to the

B-2A production complex located at Air Force Plant 42, Site 4, Palmdale, California. To the north end of the lake bed and just to the west about a mile, is what has to be the world's largest rotating antenna. It could be seen with the unaided eye over a distance of twelve to fourteen miles. It rotates at four revolutions per minute. An estimation of the antenna's dimensions is 150 feet by 450 feet. It appeared to be shaped like a very large Ballistic Missile Early Warning System (BMEWS) antenna they had along the Distant Early Warning (DEW) line in the early 1960s. M. Sgt. Bobby Sheldon, 37th FW/PA

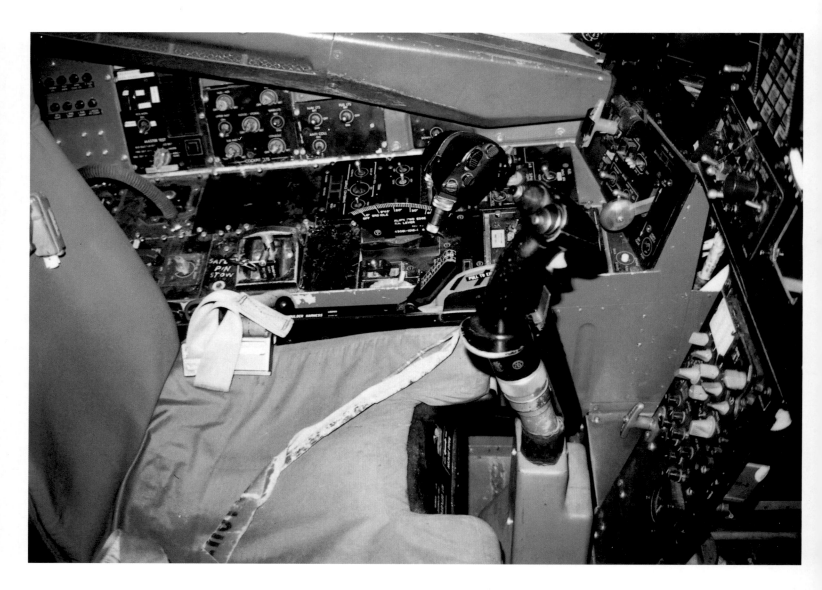

Previous page
This is the only YF-117A to be viewed by the public to date. It is the second YF-117A, serial number 78-781. It carries an ED tail code, and in place of the 37th TFW patch on either side of the intakes, it carries the patch for the Air Force Flight Test Center at Edwards Air Force Base, California. The YF-117A never operated out of Edwards, but does use the base's airspace, so it carries the ED tail code. Once it left its first home at Groom Lake, it spent the rest of its flying days operating out of Site 7, Air Force Plant 24, Palmdale, California. Dave Menard

administration had increased funding for stealth by a factor of one hundred. The bulk of that increase went into the development and production of a full-scale operational stealth aircraft, the Lockheed F-117A; code name, Senior Trend.

A close-up view of the left-side console on YF-117A number 781. Note the numerous buttons and switches on the throttles and control stick which help the pilot keep hands on the stick and throttle (HOTAS). The radios are located on the part of the instrument panel immediately in front of the control stick. Wayne Wachsmuth via Dick Cole

YF-117A

The Lockheed F-117A is a unique airplane by anyone's standards and represents the first all-out design effort to develop an operational stealth aircraft. Lockheed was successful over the years in reducing the radar signatures of their SR-71 Blackbird and worked on ways to reduce the radar cross section of the venerable U-2R and TR-1A. The strange and unusual shape of the F-117A is the direct result of this design effort and provided the Lockheed aerodynamic,

stability, and control engineers with a real challenge. The net results of these efforts were successful.

The F-117As have been operational since October 1983. They flew first with the 4450th Tactical Group out of the Groom Lake test facility and later from the Tonopah Test Range with the 37th Tactical Fighter Wing. In the early part of 1992, they were transferred to Holloman Air Force Base, New Mexico, with the 49th Fighter Wing.

The F-117A represents second generation, or late 1970s stealth technology. Industry has now learned how to round off some of the edges as is evident in the design of the Northrop B-2A, and the YF-22 and YF-23 Advanced Tactical Fighter prototypes. The low-observability characteristics of the F-117A proved that significant reductions in radar cross section plus

maintainability in the first ever operational stealth aircraft could be achieved. The F-117A is a single-place subsonic night attack aircraft powered by twin, nonafterburning General Electric F-404-F1D2 engines, similar to the engines used in the McDonnell Douglas F/A-18. The maximum gross weight is 52,500 pounds with the overall dimensions similar to that of the F-15.

The F-117A uses a wide variety of design features to reduce the aircraft radar, infrared, visual, contrail, and electromagnetic signatures. Some of the techniques used include a wing sweep of sixty-seven degrees; a faceted surface, which by design reflects 99.9 percent of the radar energy away from the receiving source; radar-absorbing structures and materials; and a gridded inlet. The gridded inlet is made of radar-absorbing material. To a hostile radar, the grid

shows up as a solid flat panel and absorbs or reflects most of the radar energy away from the source. Any radar signal that enters the inlet is reflected and bounced internally in the radar-absorbing-material-coated, S-ducted engine inlets reducing the chance of any energy being reflected out. The two high-aspect-ratio, two-dimensional exhaust nozzles, called the Platypus, flattens the exhaust plume and defuses the infrared signature to a threshold below that of most infrared detection systems' abilities to acquire and track. As with any low-observable aircraft, all weapons must be carried internally to avoid detection because they are also excellent radar reflectors, justifying the need for the F-117's large internal weapons bay. To reduce the possibility of an external antenna or transmissions giving the enemy the location of the stealth aircraft, pilots

The far side of the YF-117A instrument panel is very close in appearance to the production aircraft's. At the lower right side of panel are the warning lights for the numerous systems on the aircraft. Wayne Wachsmuth via Dick Cole

employ special retractable antennas and classified radio frequency data transmission techniques during missions into hostile air space.

All aircraft designs are a compromise of one sort or another, with the primary mission objective being the driving force in the design criteria. The primary task of the F-117A is to penetrate enemy airspace with the intent of destroying high value targets and returning unharmed and undetected.

In the design of the F-117A, one of the major challenges was to provide as much leading edge sweep as possible and

still achieve the required combat radius. This was accomplished by carrying the wing as far back as possible in order to increase the span. The trailing edge of the delta was notched out both for low-observable reasons and to reduce the wetted area.

The highly swept V-tails on the F-117A design were another concession to lower the radar signature of the aircraft. The goal was to reduce the height and size of the control surface and still provide enough control for the unstable yaw axis. Lockheed investigated several different designs such as split elevon tips but decided on the twin tail to provide the necessary control and reduced drag.

Since traditional horizontal tails were not going to be used, a set of large full-span elevons were provided for both pitch and roll control. The elevons were sized to handle the aircraft's natural pitch instability, which resulted in more roll control power than was needed.

Since this was the first airplane ever designed by electrical engineers, it was not surprising a number of aerodynamic sins were committed. In fact, the unaugmented airframe exhibits just about every mode of unstable behavior possible for an aircraft: longitudinal and directional instability, pitch up, pitch down, dihedral reversal, and various cross-axis couplings. The only thing it doesn't do is tip back on its tail when it's parked.

Because of these stability and control characteristics, there was no question as to the kind of flight control system the aircraft required. It had to be a full-time fly-by-wire command augmentation system. Any mechanical back-up system would just add weight, since the pilot control is impossible without the stability augmentation system on line.

In developing the flight control systems for the F-117A, it was decided to design the aircraft to appear to handle just like an ordinary aircraft, much like the F-4E or F-111F. This design feature

The aftmost section of the YF-117A console's left side. The red guarded switches in the lower part of the photo control the fuel transfer pumps. The two guarded switches at the top of the photo couple or decouple the airframe-mounted accessory drives (AMAD)—engine-driven generators. Wayne Wachsmuth via Dick Cole

would allow the average line pilot to fly the F-117A without extensive retraining.

The net result of this flight control development is an airplane with comparable pitch and roll response to that of a conventionally shaped fighter or attack airplane within certain boundaries. Despite press coverage to the contrary, the F-117A is maneuverable and fully aerobatic.

The F-117A's initial flight testing began with a series of flights in the Calspan NT-33 (a highly modified Lockheed T-33A outfitted with a computer-controlled variable flight management system). This program allowed Lockheed and the Air Force to iron out some of the suitability and handling problems with the F-117A fly-by-wire system. One of the variations tested assumed that the directional stability was even worse than predicted so the pilot could see the effects and get some experience.

The first flight of the first YF-117A—Air Force serial number 79-10780—took place at the Groom Lake test facility on 18 June 1981. The YF-117A's air-data probes were of a new design and had exhibited some problems during a series of ground tests, so it was decided to add some ballast to move the center of gravity as far forward as possible and make the first flight with the angle-of-attack and the yaw inputs disengaged to the main flight computer to prevent any possible problems. Special cockpit switches were incorporated so the pilot could, if necessary, reactivate the angle-of-attack and beta feedback after attaining a stabilized flight condition at 15,000 feet. Extenders were installed on those switches so they could be quickly turned on if needed. As soon as the number one YF-117A became airborne, it became apparent that the directional stability was significantly worse than predicted. The inputs to the main flight computer were activated immediately.

Much to the relief of the flight-test team, the main flight computers worked as planned. The YF-117A stabilized and the rest of the first flight was routine. This experience, once again, showed the

The aft portion of the YF-117A console's right side. The yellow and black striped handle is the manual canopy crank used to raise and lower the canopy. Wayne Wachsmuth via Dick Cole

The forward part of the console's right side. The inertial navigation system controls, IFF controls, oxygen regulator, and the environmental controls are located here. The canopy handle is visible on the right-hand sidewall. Wayne Wachsmuth via Dick Cole

value of using in-flight simulation to investigate possible aerodynamic variations prior to first flight.

Although it incorporates new technologies, the Lockheed F-117A was developed in significantly less time and for less cost than comparable fighter or

The main instrument panel of the YF-117A differs considerably from the panel of the production F-117A. Besides the absence of the twelve-by-twelve inch infrared display and the two five-inch cathode-ray-tube displays the YF-117A also has an annunciator panel for test telemetry. Wayne Wachsmuth via Dick Cole

attack aircraft. This was achieved within the tight security of a special access program using streamlined management methods. US Air Force Aeronautical Systems Division and Lockheed Skunk Works personnel worked in a nonadversarial problem-solving atmosphere with a minimum number of people. In addition, the use of proven components from other aircraft reduced the risk and gave Lockheed the confidence to begin production concurrently with development.

In November 1978, the Air Force contracted with Lockheed for the full-scale development program of the F-117A. The first flight flew only thirty-one months after contract go-ahead. Lockheed signed a fixed price production contract eighteen months before the first flight date, January 1980. With production concurrence, the F-117A achieved Initial Operational Capability in October 1983, only twenty-eight months from the date of the first flight. On 3 July 1990, the last of fifty-nine production F-117As were delivered to the US Air Force's Tactical Air Command. This marked an end to the F-117A production. As of this writing, both congress and the Air Force have decided not to proceed with follow-on production. It was hoped that at least twenty-four additional aircraft would be contracted for with an additional

This view of the F-117A shows off the forward-looking infrared (FLIR) in the on configuration. Just under the canopy is the large primary element of the FLIR with the laser bore sight being the smaller of the three circles. The FLIR system is the primary target identification system on the F-117A. The FLIR also provides a video image to the pilot during taxi and takeoff on blacked-out airfields, enabling him to find his way without the aid of external lights. Visible on either side of the cockpit are the twin retractable ILS (instrument landing system) antenna. James C. Goodall

During the first public showing of the F-117A, Lt. Col. Ralph Getchell raises the large F-117A canopy. In looking closer, it becomes apparent that on the F-117A there are a minimum of straight edges on any leading edge surface. Even the canopy edges are faceted. The F-117A's cockpit is large and roomy when compared to other modern single-place aircraft. Two hydraulic rams, one on either side of the ACES II ejection seat raise the canopy. Note the wide forward instrument panel, the size of the head-up display, and the pilot's all-black helmet. James C. Goodall

eighteen to twenty-four aircraft designated for the British Royal Air Force.

The total development cost to the Air Force for the Senior Trend program was just under $2 billion. This included low-observable technology development, the full-scale development aircraft comprising five airframes, follow-on development upgrades, and all subcontractor and Air Force related costs.

Despite the extremely low production rate of only eight aircraft in its best year, the average flyaway cost of the F-117A for the fifty-nine production aircraft came to just under $43 million, including all government supplied equipment. The government supplied equipment consisted of the off-the-shelf electronics (such as the F-16 flight

computers), the General Electric jet engines, and a host of the electronic black boxes. The total program cost was just over $6.5 billion, which included everything from the $600 million to build the air base facility at the Tonopah Test Range site to all fifty-nine F-117As and five YF-117As. These costs compare favorably with other new aircraft programs.

The F-117A again demonstrates that the Lockheed Skunk Works method is still the way to get what you want, when you want it, at a reasonable cost.

The F-117A Becomes Operational

With the successful end of the Have Blue program and the issuance of a full-

scale development contract to Lockheed, it became time to select the operational pilots.

The first operational pilots were selected in 1980. They came from the ranks of early- to mid-career captains with a thousand or more hours of jet time. The profile was almost identical for all the pilots chosen: air-to-ground F-4, F-111, A-10, or A-7 experience. During the initial interviews, the potential candidates were given approximately five minutes to say yes or no to a program that was still so black that they wouldn't have even the faintest idea of what they had gotten themselves into for two more years. All they knew was that at some time in the future they would be notified, but until then it was back to their normal assignments.

Two years after the initial interviews, the first group of seventeen Air Force pilots reported to Nellis Air Force Base, Nevada. The unit was called the 4450th Tactical Group flying A-7Ds as a cover aircraft. (In this first group of pilots was a young major named Alton Whitley; almost ten years later, Col. Alton Whitley commanded the 37th Tactical Fighter

Wing and their F-117s into battle over the skies of Baghdad.)

One of the first tasks of this newly formed group was to develop training programs for the pilots who would follow in the years to come and operational patterns that would last until 10 November 1989.

In mid-1982, the F-117A began the transition from the Groom Lake test facility—sometimes called the "Ranch," "Dream Land," "Area 51," or "The Site"— to the new base that was still under construction at the former Sandia weapons facility known as the Tonopah Test Range, (TTR).

After the delivery of the fifteenth production airplane, Air Force serial number 82-0799, on 28 October 1983, the 4450th Tactical Group was declared operational at Tonopah. The date was significant because it was just before the 4450th Tactical Group was declared operational that the first combat mission was considered.

Operational pilots commuted weekly from Nellis Air Force Base to Tonopah. They arrived on a government-chartered Boeing 727 or 737 on Monday and left by noon that following Friday.

This view shows the F-117A's long thin exhaust duct. The upward-swept platypus shields the exhaust from view below and to the rear of the F-117A, reducing the chance of infrared detection. From the viewpoint of enemy fighters trying to secure an infrared lock on the F-117A, this type of exhaust ejector makes their job very difficult. James C. Goodall

Monday was considered a light-duty day, but Tuesday through Thursday had a full flying schedule of up to two sorties per night.

The nighttime sorties were quite demanding because they lasted one and a half hours with missions being flown over much of the western United States. The routes flown took the aircraft up to the Lake Tahoe, Nevada, area to the eastern edge of the Wendover range over Utah, up through the Mountain Home bombing range in south central Idaho, and into the China Lake and Edwards Air Force Base range in California. When they returned from a night of flying, the pilots went through a debrief with maintenance and with the mission planners, whose task was to evaluate the pilots' adherence to

31

the mission profile. The day typically ended with the last crew debrief between 0300 and 0430 hours.

F-117As Prepare for War

In response to the destruction of the Marine barracks in Beirut, Lebanon, in October 1983, the Department of Defense seriously considered a surprise attack on the terrorists that were responsible for the bombing. US and Israeli intelligence knew the whereabouts of the terrorist team in southern Lebanon. The US Navy's Seventh Fleet was prepositioned off the coast of Lebanon. The F/A-18s and A-6Es of the carrier battle group were put on alert and told to be ready to launch with minimum notice. The Navy brass was briefed as to the possible targets located in south central Lebanon. Stateside, the 4450th's F-117As had been alerted with about ten aircraft armed, inertial navigation systems aligned, flight crews

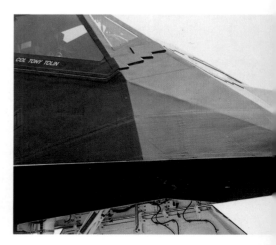

The twin weapons bay doors are on the bottom of the aircraft fuselage and are hinged to open along the aircraft's centerline. Just forward of each weapons door are two extended spoilers that reduce buffeting during weapons separation. The weapons pylon is only extended during load and unload of weapons or the universal aircraft travel pod. James C. Goodall

A good view showing the four static pitot tubes used on the F-117A. James C. Goodall

Aircraft 85-0836, the fifty-second F-117A, delivered to the Air Force on 19 October 1988, prepares for roll-out of its hangar at Tonopah. Every hangar at Tonopah has an American flag hanging from its ceiling. Also located above the aircraft is the extensive air-conditioning system needed to keep the Black Jet cool in the hot desert sun. Lockheed

briefed, with standby aircrews and maintenance crews prepared for their first overseas deployment.

Their flight plan would take them from Tonopah, accompanied by four to six KC-135A tankers from either Beale Air Force Base, California, or March Air Force Base, California, to Myrtle Beach Air Force Base, North Carolina, under the cover of darkness. They were to be put into hangars immediately after landing. Each F-117A would receive a complete postflight inspection, and the best four

A night view of an F-117A in its hangar, illuminated by only the hangar lights. Lockheed

aircraft prepared for the fifteen-hour flight to southern Lebanon. Retaliation for the deaths of 241 American servicemen in Beirut was about to begin.

With less than an hour to go before the first F-117A launch from Tonopah, Caspar Weinberger (then secretary of defense) decided that attacking another country was not the proper thing to do. He scrubbed the mission of both the 4450th and the aircraft of the Seventh Fleet. The F-117As were taken off their alert status, disarmed, and reprogrammed for training flights.

Operation Eldorado Canyon

In April 1986, officials again considered using the F-117A. Lockheed had delivered the thirty-third aircraft (85-0817) to the Air Force giving the 4450th Tactical Group two full squadrons of Stealth Fighters.

Col. Muammar Gaddafi, Libya's leader, had been engaged in a saber rattling contest with the US Navy for over a year. He set up his "line of death" across the Gulf of Sidra and dared the United States to cross it, threatening to destroy any ship or aircraft that tried. After a

F-117A number 81-10793, the ninth production aircraft, readies for a night training mission from its secured hangar at Tonopah. The two crew members to the rear of the aircraft are about to remove the wheel chocks, while the crew chief signals the pilot to apply his brakes. Lockheed

brief turkey shoot in which Navy F-14 Tomcats shot down two Libyan Su-22 fighters, the United States decided enough was enough—time to strike back.

Previous page
A KC-135A/Q refuels an F-117A in the Nevada desert sky, silhouetted by the setting sun. Lockheed

Under the cover of darkness, on the night of 15 April 1986, the bombing raid on Libya, code-named Operation Eldorado Canyon was about to begin. Once more, the capabilities of the F-117A made it the weapons system best suited for the job. Senior staff at Tactical Air Command headquarters knew the F-117A could do the job and had put the 4450th Tactical Group on alert for possible deployment to the Mediterranean for the specific purpose of bombing Libya. As with the raid on Lebanon in October 1983, Caspar Weinberger would not commit the F-117A to combat because he felt that the aircraft was too valuable to risk on such an insignificant target. The alert was called off with less than one hour to initial launch from Tonopah. The raid was conducted by US Air Force F-111s flying from bases in England and US Navy carrier aircraft. Col. Muammar

The off-base housing facility for the Tonopah Test Range can best be described as an exercise in defining the true meaning of the term "in the middle of nowhere." The base is approximately 185 air miles north-northwest of Las Vegas, Nevada, and as the crow flies, thirty-five miles from the town of Tonopah, Nevada. James C. Goodall

Previous page
A fine look-down view with the sun at low angles shows off the true shape of this very special aircraft. This shot was taken over the north end of the Salton Sea near the town of Imperial, California. Lockheed

Gaddafi has not been a major threat since.

F-117 Goes into Combat

Operation Just Cause was the first use of the F-117A in a "combat" role— although there was no air defense network or air-to-air threat within 1,000

A view of Half Dome in the Yosemite Valley is the backdrop of this view of F-117A number 82-0802. Lockheed

An F-117A being refueled over the Nellis test range by a March Air Force Base, California, based KC-10A Extender. Upward visibility from the F-117A is limited so air refueling is difficult until the pilot has mastered the technique. Lockheed

miles. Even so, the Pentagon planners felt they had to do something to justify the program, and a very limited threat environment with a good chance of success was the way to go. On the night of 9 December 1989 the F-117As dropped real bombs on real targets. Only four

GBU-27 bombs were dropped during the raid, and one missed its target by as much as 1,000 yards. The miss was attributed to poor coordination between Army and Air Force planners. It would be another twenty-three months before the Lockheed Black Jet would prove to the world, and Saddam Hussein, its worth as the world's best tactical strike bomber in Operation Desert Storm.

As the program developed and more aircraft were delivered to the 4450th Tactical Group, the force grew to three squadrons: The 415th Tactical Fighter Squadron "Nightstalkers," the 416th

Tactical Fighter Squadron "Ghost Riders," and the 417th Tactical Fighter Squadron "Bandits."

In October 1989 the 37th Tactical Fighter Wing at George Air Force Base, California, was deactivated and reactivated as an operational wing flying the F-117A, replacing the newly deactivated 4450th Tactical Group. The three squadrons were redesignated the 415th Tactical Fighter Squadron, the 416th Tactical Fighter Squadron, and the 417th Tactical Fighter Training Squadron. Each squadron consisted of eighteen aircraft with the exception of the 417th.

37th Tactical Fighter Wing assigned ground crewmen pull the chocks from the main landing as the taxi director signals the pilot to hold his position. From below or directly behind, the exhaust ejectors are not visible. Lockheed

A pair of F-117As taxi out for a night of flying over the Nevada desert. The small bulges on the right side of both aircraft are detachable radar reflectors, installed so the local air-traffic-control radars and other radars can track the F-117A. Lockheed

Typically ten to twelve F-117As are undergoing periodic depot maintenance at either Site 7 in Air Force Plant 42 at Palmdale, California, or on site at Tonopah. This left six to ten aircraft for the 417th Tactical Fighter Training Squadron.

The best shot ever taken of the bottom of an F-117A according to the Skunk Works' chief photographer Denny Lombard. This is not a Lockheed shot, but one that Tony Landis took on a trip we made to the Tonopah fence line on 14 and 15 September 1991. On that same trip, we observed the launch of twenty-four F-117As in one hour and twenty minutes. The other significance of this photo is the first shot of a WA coded F-117A, tail number 82-0804, delivered to the Air Force on 20 June 1984. This was the last F-117A of the initial batch. Tony Landis

F-117A number 81-10796 on final approach to the Tonopah Test Range. Just under the tail of the F-117A is the housing facility for everyone assigned to Tonopah. The northern fence line is the line that runs almost top to bottom just to the left of the aircraft's left wing tip. It is from this fence line that Tony Landis, John Andrews (Testor Model Company), and I have viewed and photographed F-117As since the winter of 1988. Lockheed

The F-117A instructor pilots fly chase in these TR coded T-38As painted in three-tone gray. The unit has eight of these chase planes assigned to the 417th Tactical Fighter Training Squadron, based at Tonopah. This aircraft is still marked in the 4450th Tactical Group markings. Photo taken on 19 July 1989. Marty Isham

Before the F-117A unit at both Groom Lake and Tonopah received their T-38As, they flew the A-7D carrying the LV tail code. By mid-1989 most of the A-7Ds were replaced by Northrop T-38As. Kevin Patrick

Prior to the official announcement and government acknowledgment of the existence of the F-117A, all flying operations were conducted under the cover of darkness. The hangar doors could not even be opened until thirty minutes after official sunset. This posed a problem for first-time F-117A pilots. Their first F-117A flight was made at night. Because of the extreme secrecy surrounding the project, daytime flying could only be conducted at the Groom Lake test facility.

The Air Force will never completely declassify the program because it is a covert-operations aircraft. As it turns out, the program is more classified today than it was when the F-117As first started flying over ten years ago. It was designed from the onset for use supporting other covert organizations such as DELTA (the US Army's elite counterterrorist force), specifically for first-strike capabilities, and built with the idea it could overfly any country's airspace, at will, without detection. It was designed to operate in

F-117A number 84-0828 lands at Nellis Air Force Base, Nevada, during its first public press conference. The drag chute is always used on the F-117A and comes in three basic colors: black as shown in the photo, nomex green, and light yellow. James C. Goodall

An Air Force security policeman guards an F-117A on the Nellis ramp during the official roll-out on 21 April 1990. James C. Goodall

For the first time since they joined the program, pilots and maintenance personnel could have a "hero" photo in front of the formerly super-secret Black Jet. James C. Goodall

conditions exactly like those experienced over Baghdad in Operation Desert Storm: attacking highly defended, hardened, fixed targets such as command and control centers, command communications facilities, missile

F-117A number 84-0820 is lost in a sea of 37th Tactical Fighter Wing family and friends at the first public showing of the F-117A. To many of the family members who had loved ones working on the F-117A, this was the end of the official veil of secrecy that had kept the wing's members from telling or describing just what they had been working on all these years. James C. Goodall

storage bunkers, and high-threat air defense installations.

The F-117A was never intended to be used in large numbers; the mission profile calls for a "lone wolf" approach to the target area. Even though there were as many as thirty-five F-117As over the skies of Baghdad on any given night during Operation Desert Storm, the mission was to fly alone, in total silence, under the cover of darkness.

F-117A Goes Public

After the 10 November 1989 public announcement and the lifting of the daytime flying restrictions, the 417th Tactical Fighter Training Squadron started flying three to four times a day. Usually a cell of three F-117As flew during each of the daytime missions, almost always followed by a T-38A chase plane.

Operation Desert Storm

On 2 August 1990 Iraqi leader Saddam Hussein gave the order to invade the Persian Gulf kingdom of Kuwait. The response from the United States was the beginning of the largest build-up of US military personnel and machines since the Vietnam War. The purpose of the build-up was to prevent the Iraqis from taking control of the entire Arabian peninsula. US and allied intelligence operations all came to the same conclusion: If the United Nations did not respond to the invasion of Kuwait, then that would give a signal to Iraq that they could take the entire Middle East unopposed. Once the Iraqi army had secured the country of Kuwait, their next targets were Saudi Arabia, the United Arab Emirates, Bahrain, and Oman until they joined up with Yemen. If the world

Aircraft number 84-0812 flies in formation with a KC-135Q tanker out of Beale Air Force Base, California, on its way to the Middle East via Langley Air Force Base, Virginia. Mike Dornheim, Aviation Week & Space Technology

had allowed that to happen, Saddam Hussein would have gained control of over sixty percent of the free world's oil, a frightening prospect, indeed.

Until the deployment of the F-117A and its trial by fire over the skies of Baghdad, no one, except a handful of key Lockheed, Department of Defense, and Air Force brass, knew of this incredible aircraft's capabilities.

On 19 August 1990 twenty-two F-117As from the 415th Tactical Fighter Squadron, accompanied by a dozen

A view of Capt. Dave Francis' F-117A coming in for a drink, as viewed from the boom operators position on the KC-135Q. The first squadron of F-117As to be deployed to Saudi Arabia was midway across the United States when this photo was taken. In the flight were twenty-two F-117As on the way to Langley. During the flight, five retractable antennas were observed in the extended position—one large and one small blade antenna on the top of the aircraft and one large and two small antennas on the bottom. The radar reflectors on the side of the fuselage have been removed. Mike Dornheim, *Aviation Week & Space Technology*

KC-135 tankers out of Beale Air Force Base, California, flew nonstop from the Tonopah Test Range to the headquarters of the Tactical Air Command, Langley Air Force Base, Virginia. After a crew rest, postflight and preflight inspections, twenty of the twenty-two F-117As, accompanied by a flight of Air Force KC-10A tankers headed out on 20 August for the fifteen-hour flight to King Khaid Air Base near the city of Khamis Mushait, Saudi Arabia. The two spare F-117As were sent back to Tonopah to wait their turn.

The base and the facility in Saudi Arabia were built by the Saudis in the

F-117A banks over the central farmlands of the Midwest after taking on fuel from a KC-135Q tanker. Mike Dornheim, *Aviation Week & Space Technology*

early 1980s to fulfill an Air Force requirement for a forward operating location for a then-undefined strike aircraft. This requirement was fulfilled as part of the deal that allowed the Saudis to purchase F-15A and F-15B Eagles and the E-3A Airborne Warning and Control System (AWACS) aircraft from the US

First F-117A lands at Langley Air Force Base on 19 August 1990 on the first leg of its trip to Saudi Arabia. USAF

After touchdown, the first F-117A pops its black breaking chute on the Langley runway.

Note the F-15 on alert in the hangar in the background. USAF

government in the early 1980s—over strong Israeli objections.

King Khaid Air Base was designed specifically for the F-117A, and its facilities had not been used before the first detachment of F-117As arrived in August. In fact, 415th Tactical Fighter Squadron personnel had to break airtight seals when they first entered the buildings and hangars. Each underground hangar could house two F-117As with all their support equipment and had an air purification system that would keep out all known nuclear, biological, and chemical agents, huge blast doors that could take a direct hit from anything the Iraqis could throw at them, and underground revetments and taxiways. The parking aprons were below normal ground level requiring pinpoint bombing from any enemy that hoped to destroy the F-117s. And the attacking aircraft would still have to fly over and through 600 miles of Saudi airspace to escape.

The housing facilities were four-bedroom units housing twenty to twenty-two persons per unit. All members lived and worked in air conditioned comfort, and for their time-off periods they had a swimming pool.

By the middle of November, it became apparent that the Iraqi military was not going to leave Kuwait voluntarily. With that thought, President George Bush made the decision to escalate the war effort by dramatically increasing the number of troops committed to Operation Desert Shield from approximately 150,000 to approximately 450,000. The complement of allied aircraft grew to 2,500. The battle for Kuwait was just around the corner.

In this second phase of the fighting equipment build-up came the order to transfer the second squadron of F-117As from Tonopah to Saudi Arabia. The 416th Tactical Fighter Squadron was called up December 4, 1990, their twenty-three Stealth Fighters joining the twenty already in-country. This deployment left three F-117As Stateside for training or replacement if needed.

The largest gathering of Black Jets outside of Tonopah. Lined up on the Langley ramp for the whole world to see are twenty-two of the fifty-six F-117As. USAF

Located at King Khaid Air Base, Saudi Arabia, an F-117A from the 37th Tactical Fighter Wing sits in the noon sun parked in a reveted taxiway. USAF

Desert Storm Begins

At approximately 1500 hours Washington, D.C., time on 16 January 1991, thirty-one F-117As from the 415th and 416th Tactical Fighter Squadrons, led by Col. Alton Whitley, commander of the 37th Tactical Fighter Wing, entered Iraqi airspace en route to downtown Baghdad. At that same time, Operation Desert Shield became Operation Desert Storm. The move to free Kuwait from the grip of

Parked in the reveted parking apron, three F-117As undergo postflight inspection during the training phase of Operation Desert Shield. USAF

Col. Alton Whitley, commander of the 37th Tactical Fighter Wing, poses in front of an F-117A at Tonopah East, Saudi Arabia. While still a major, Whitley was the first Air Force pilot to fly the F-117A. His first flight was in 1981 at the Groom Lake test facility in the Nevada desert. USAF

the Iraqi invaders began in earnest. Operation Desert Storm became the largest aerial bombing campaign in the history of modern warfare. On the first night of the bombing of Kuwait and Iraq, more than 1,000 sorties were flown. It was also the first time that a manned Stealth aircraft was used as a frontline weapon.

An F-117A, number 85-0818, of the 415th Tactical Fighter Squadron sits patiently in the brand new shelters at King Khaid Air Base, which were built specifically for the F-117As by the Saudi government in the 1980s. USAF

The F-117As from the 37th Tactical Fighter Wing were the only manned aircraft allowed to overfly Baghdad, reported to be the most heavily defended airspace in the world.

On the first day of Desert Storm, the F-117As from King Khaid Air Base dropped sixty-two 2,000-pound laser-guided bombs squarely on the most critical targets of the Iraqi military: key Iraqi air defense complexes, command and control centers, Scud surface-to-surface missile storage bunkers, and the

most impressive hit of the early air campaign, the headquarters of the Iraqi air force. The image of that 2,000-pound laser-guided bomb flying down the elevator shaft of the building, hitting the basement and blowing all four walls out is one of the most significant aerial bombardment films ever.

The F-117As flew 1,261 sorties and destroyed over sixty percent of the strategic targets. Each F-117A sortie averaged six hours. They flew a total of 7,550 hours of combat time without a single loss of an aircraft or crew member and, even more incredible, not one F-117A was damaged even though they flew through some of the most intense antiaircraft artillery (triple-A) and surface-to-air missile (SAM) defenses that any pilot or plane has *ever* flown

through. The six weeks of Operation Desert Storm proved beyond a doubt that the men and women of the Lockheed Advanced Development Company, along with its now retired president, Ben R. Rich, had built the most capable surgical strike aircraft in the history of modern warfare. They did this ahead of schedule, under budget, all while under the wraps of total secrecy over a ten-year period. No other company in the free world could have done what Rich and his team did— not even close.

SQN LDR GRAHAM WARDELL

SSGT CHUCK MATSON
SSGT BILL DOOM
SGT JIM BANAS
SGT LEE KINGSLEY

Previous page
Another view of the parking ramp at King Khaid Air Base. The F-117A closest to the camera bears the name of Royal Air Force Squadron Leader Graham Wardell. (The US Air Force and Royal Air Force regularly exchange pilots. Squadron Leader Wardell flew combat missions with the US Air Force during Desert Storm.) The crew members are S. Sgt. Chuck Matson, S. Sgt. Bill Doom, Sgt. Jim Banas and Sgt. Lee Kingslee. USAF

A family portrait of the 415th Tactical Fighter Squadron members taken in Saudi Arabia prior to Desert Storm. USAF

An F-117A parked in a protected revetment at King Khaid Air Base. After Desert Storm began, ground crewmen started painting one small GBU-27 Paveway III stencil for each mission under the aircraft's left side just under the canopy rail. USAF

This photo was taken through a starlight low-light, night-vision scope from the boom operators station of a KC-135 tanker. All that can really be made out are the wing tip formation lights, the inlet observation lights, and the heat from the exhaust ejector platypus. USAF

This once-in-a-lifetime opportunity occurred on 1 April 1991 when the 37th Tactical Fighter Wing had its Homecoming from Operation Desert Storm at Nellis Air Force Base. Seven of the eight F-117As are visible in this view. The aircraft tail numbers are: 813 (not shown), 830, 810, 814, 808, 825, 791, and the last production F-117A, 843. James C. Goodall

Black Assassin, *F-117A number 85-0830,
taxis to the Nellis ramp area after the one-
stop trip from Saudi Arabia. The doors just
in front of the V tail are the parachute doors.*

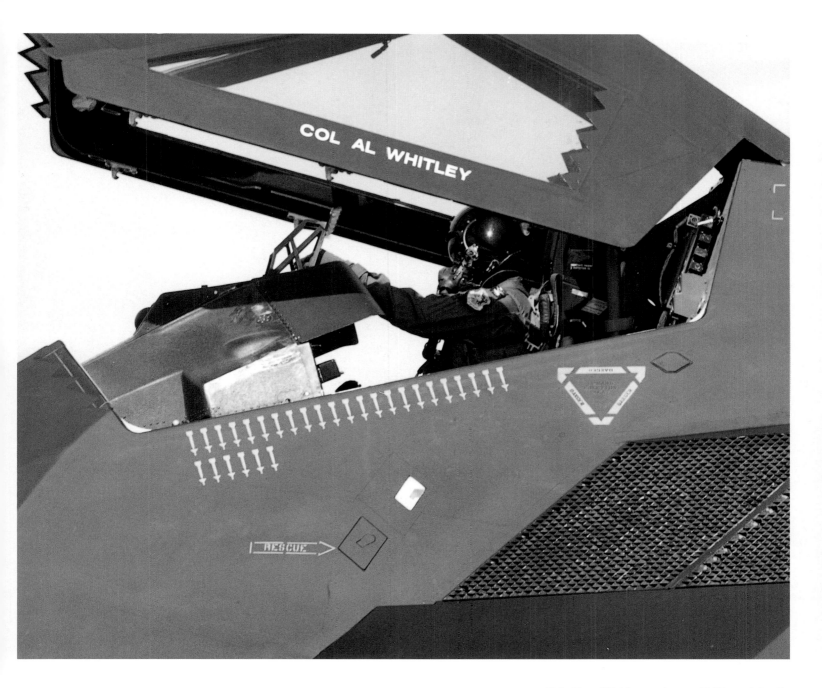

COL AL WHITLEY

RESCUE

Col. Alton Whitley arrives at Nellis on 1 April 1991 after a total of 220 days in the southwestern desert of Saudi Arabia and over the skies of Baghdad, Iraq. This aircraft carries twenty-nine mission markings represented by GBU-27 bomb silhouettes under the cockpit opening. The white diamond-shaped device below the mission marking is used to illuminate the inlet grid to inspect the inlet for icing. James C. Goodall

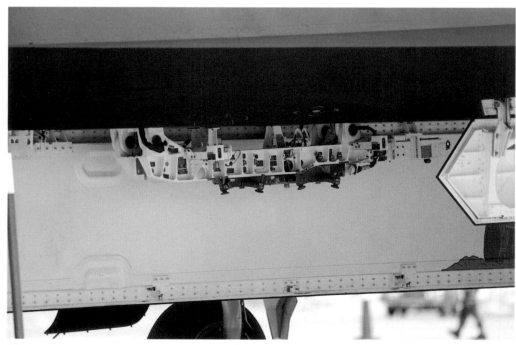

Whitley's F-117A, The Toxic Avenger, *number 813, with its weapons bay doors open and the weapons pylon's in the lowered position. Just above the head of the* The Toxic Avenger *is a normally retracted UHF antenna. The weapons pylon would be extended during flight only if the F-117A were employing target-acquiring weapons, such as the infrared-guided Maverick or the Hughes AIM-120 Advanced Medium Range Air-to-Air Missile (AMRAAM).*

Another view of the weapons pylon without travel pod. In examining the eight aircraft that came into Nellis on 1 April 1991, there were two different types of pylons, presumably for different types of weapons.

Thor, *number 808, still has the old-style weapons bay doors. The Air Force has instituted a program to retrofit all F-117As with the new doors before the end of 1992.*

The weapons bay door on number 791 is a new style, all-composite door that is stronger than the original metal door. The composite doors can both be opened for dual weapons release, whereas only one metal door could be open at a time.

Festivities over, the eight F-117As head back to Tonopah and a long awaited welcome home by their families and friends. For the record, the Air Force wasn't so cruel as to have the men who had just flown in from a five-month deployment turn around and fly their F-117As back to Tonopah. The 37th Tactical Fighter Wing had replacement aircrews ready to ferry the birds back. James C. Goodall

By the end of summer 1992, all F-117As will be relocated from the remote operations of the Tonopah Test Range to Holloman Air Force Base, New Mexico. With this change of bases comes a change in command: the F-117As will now fly under the command of the 49th Fighter Wing, and the 415th, 416th, and 417th Fighter Squadrons will carry over from the 37th Tactical Fighter Wing days. The photo shows an HO coded F-117A seen at Holloman in mid-December 1991. Roy Pruitt

Next page
The latest F-117A unit markings: instead of carrying 37th TFW the new designation is 37th FW. This is the first time I've seen tail number 82-0800; it is the sixteenth F-117A, delivered to the Air Force on 7 December 1983. This photo was taken at the Tactical Air Command commanders conference at Tyndall Air Force Base, Florida, on 2 November 1991. 1st Lt. Chris Mayer, USAF

The Northrop B-2A Stealth Bomber

The B-2 Advanced Technology Bomber began to take form during 1979 design studies at Northrop. Within a week of the studies, it became apparent that the winning design would be that of the flying wing. The original shape was more of a true diamond-shaped vehicle with an extremely small side-view cross section. Within the center section would be four nonafterburning jet engines, a single large bomb bay, and a center cockpit crew section.

Northrop was back in the flying wing business after an absence of over thirty-five years.

The first Northrop flying wings of the 1940s suffered from dramatic control problems that resulted in the loss of the YB-49A in the late forties. To overcome this barrier, the Advanced Technology Bomber would incorporate a computer-controlled fly-by-wire flight control system. Like the wings of the 1940s, the Advanced Technology Bomber would use a combination of elevon-like control surfaces and "split-drag rudders" to control pitch, roll, and yaw. Everything would be controlled by a quad-redundant fly-by-wire flight control system designed

Roll-out day for the prototype Northrop B-2A Stealth Bomber. The roll-out occurred on 22 November 1988 at Air Force Plant 42, Site 4, Palmdale, California. Just in front of the B-2A is a stylized star made up of five B-2A silhouettes. Northrop

to monitor all elements of the wing, in real time.

In a 22 August 1980 statement Harold Brown, then secretary of defense, officially acknowledged the existence of American Stealth technology programs, including the Advanced Technology Bomber program.

I am announcing today a major technological advance of great military significance.

This so-called stealth technology enables the United States to build manned and unmanned aircraft that cannot be successfully intercepted with existing air defense systems. We have demonstrated to our satisfaction that the technology works.

This achievement will be a formidable instrument of peace. It promises to add a unique dimension to our tactical forces and the deterrent strength of our strategic forces. At the same time it will provide us capabilities that are wholly consistent with our pursuit of verifiable arms control agreements, in particular, with the provisions of SALT [Strategic Arms Limitation Treaty] II.

For three years, we have successfully maintained the security of this program. This is because of the conscientious efforts of the relatively few people in the executive branch and the legislative branch who were briefed on the activity and of the contractors working on it. However, in the last few months, the circle of people knowledgeable about the program has widened, partly because of the increased size of the effort, and partly because of the debate underway in

congress on the new bomber proposals. Regrettably, there have been several leaks about the stealth program in the last few days in the press and television news coverage.

In the face of these leaks, I believe that it is not appropriate or creditable for us to deny the existence of this program. And it is now important to correct some of the leaked information that misrepresented the administration's position on the new bomber program. The so-called Stealth Bomber program was not a factor in our decision in 1977 to cancel the B-1; indeed, it was not yet a design.

I am gratified that, as yet, none of the most sensitive and significant classified information about the characteristics of this program has been disclosed. An important objective of the announcement today is to make clear the kinds of information that we intend scrupulously to protect at the highest security level. Dr. Perry, my under secretary of defense for research and engineering and chief architect of this program, will elaborate this point further.

In sum, we have developed a new technology of extraordinary military significance. We are vigorously applying this technology to develop a number of military aircraft and these programs are showing very great promise.

We can take tremendous pride in this latest achievement of American technology. It can play a major role in strengthening our strategic and tactical forces without in any way endangering any of our arms control initiatives. And it can contribute to the maintenance of peace by posing a new and significant offset to the

The third B-2A, serial number 82-1068. This aircraft was on public display at the Edwards Air Force Base Open House in the fall of 1991. This is a full production configuration aircraft complete with all mission avionics and related subsystems. From this view the control surfaces on the right wing are visible and in the static or nonpowered resting mode. With the control surfaces in the relaxed state, the amount of trailing edge control surface the B-2A has is evident. Tony Landis

Soviet Union's attempt to gain military ascendancy by weight of numbers.

I would like to ask Bill Perry to give you some additional details on our stealth program.

William Perry's comments were:
World War II demonstrated the decisive role that air power can play in military operations. It also demonstrated the potential of radar as a primary means of detecting aircraft and directing fire against them. On balance, though, the advantage

clearly was with the aircraft. Subsequent to World War II, defensive missiles—both ground launched and air launched—were developed and "married" with radar fire control systems. This substantially increased the effectiveness of air defense systems, shifting the balance against aircraft. For the last few decades we have been working on techniques to defeat such air defense systems. At present, our military aircraft make substantial use of electronic countermeasures [jamming] and

flying low to place themselves in ground clutter, both of which degrade the effectiveness of air defense radars. By these means we have maintained the effectiveness of our military aircraft in the face of radar-directed defensive missiles.

However, the Soviets continue to place very heavy emphasis on the development and deployment of air defense missiles in an attempt to offset the advantage we have in air power. They have built thousands of surface-to-air missile systems, they have employed radars with high power and monopulse tracking circuits which are very difficult to jam, and in the last few years they have developed air-to-air

A lineup of four B-2As. Noteworthy is the coloring of the composite material skin prior to the application of the radar absorption material and paint. There is extensive use of protective covering during the manufacturing process, and workers wear special cotton socks over their shoes.
Northrop

Shown is a family portrait of the first three B-2As, serial numbers 82-1066, 82-1067, and 82-1068, in final assembly at the Northrop Palmdale production facility. All three aircraft are covered with a white protective paper material prior to being painted. Northrop

missiles guided by look-down radars which are capable of tracking aircraft in "ground clutter."

Because of these developments and because of the importance we attach to maintaining our air superiority, we have for years been developing what we call penetration technology; the technology that degrades the effectiveness of radars and other sensors used by air defense systems. A particular emphasis has been on developing that technology which makes an aircraft "invisible" to radar. In the early 1960s, we applied a particular version of this technology to some of our reconnaissance aircraft. In the mid-1970s we applied it to the cruise missiles then being developed [Tomahawk and Boeing

Air Launched Cruise Missile]. By the summer of 1977 it became clear that this technology could be considerably extended in its effectiveness and could be applied to a wide class of vehicles including manned aircraft. We concluded that it was possible to build aircraft so difficult to detect that they could not be successfully engaged by existing air defense systems. Recognizing the great significance of such a development we took three related actions. First a ten-fold increase in our investment to advance this technology. Second we initiated a number of very high priority programs to apply this technology. And third, we gave the entire program extraordinary security protection, even to the point of classifying the very existence of such a program.

Initially we were able to limit the knowledge of the program to a very few government officials in both the executive and legislative branches and succeeded in maintaining complete secrecy about the program. However as the program increased in size—currently the annual funding is one hundred times greater than

when we decided to accelerate the program in 1977—it became necessary to brief more people. The existence of a stealth program has now become public knowledge. But even as we acknowledge the existence of a stealth program, we will draw a new security line to protect that information about the program which could facilitate a Soviet countermeasures program. We will continue to protect at the highest security level information about:

a. The specific techniques which we employ to reduce detectability
b. The degree of success of each of these techniques
c. Characteristics of the specific vehicles being developed
d. Funds being applied to specific programs
e. Schedules of specific programs

With those ground rules, I think you can see that I am extremely limited in what I can tell you about the program. I will say this. First, stealth technology does not involve a single technical approach, but rather a complex synthesis of many. Even if I were willing to describe it to you, I

could not do it in a sentence or even a paragraph. Second, while we have made remarkable advances in the technology in the last three years, we have been building on excellent work done in our defense technology program over the last two decades. Third, this technology—theoretically at least—could be applied to any military vehicle which can be attacked by radar-directed fire. We are considering all such applications which are the most practical and which have the greatest military significance. Fourth, we have achieved excellent success on the program, including tests of a number of different vehicles.

The US defense community as a whole has been studying the technologies of low-observable designs

The first two B-2As, 82-1066 on the left and 82-1067 on the right. The photo was taken at the Edwards B-2A test facility. Both aircraft are physically identical, with the exception of test equipment carried internally. As of this writing, a fourth B-2A has joined the B-2A Test Force at Edwards. Northrop

The first high-speed taxi test at Palmdale. Both sets of trailing edge control surfaces are in the lowered position, with the innermost flaps lowered to about twenty-five degrees, while the outboard flaps are lowered about twenty degrees. Northrop

for decades. Even before the Department of Defense acknowledged the key players in both the F-117A and the B-2A bomber programs, it didn't take a rocket scientist

to deduce that stealth projects were probably under way at the Lockheed Skunk Works, the Boeing Advanced Design Center, and the Building 100 complex at General Dynamics, Fort Worth, Texas.

The primary focus of stealth design has been to make aircraft difficult to detect and track by radar. The air defense system technologies of the former Soviet Union have been exported to every corner of the world, and even with the

demise of the USSR, the need to penetrate hostile air space, as was so well proven over the skies of Baghdad, still exists today and will well into the twenty-first century.

The Advanced Technology Bomber design has been optimized to represent the smallest radar target possible. When used in conjunction with other low-observable technologies, this fourth-generation stealth aircraft makes it almost impossible to track continuously

using radar. Even if a ground-based radar could track the new bomber, its radar-guided weapons could not acquire or lock-on to the target.

Stealth dramatically degrades the effectiveness of all three of the basic air defense functions—surveillance, fire control, and kill—thereby increasing the aircraft's survivability.

With the election of Ronald Reagan as President in 1980, the Carter administration's Advanced Technology Bomber program came head to head with Reagan's campaign promise to revive the canceled B-1A program for funds and presidential support. In the same time frame, congressional support for bomber programs in general was at an all-time low. How would congress fund two bomber programs, the modernized B-1A—to be called B-1B—and the Advanced Technology Bomber? Congress would have to work out a way to pay for both programs.

On 20 October 1981, Caspar Weinberger, secretary of defense for the Reagan administration announced a compromise. The Rockwell B-1B would

be built in a limited production run of 100 or fewer aircraft so funding could be provided for the Advanced Technology Bomber. The contract for the bomber would go to Northrop and its subcontractor group made up of Boeing and Ling Temco Vought (LTV). The sum of $7.3 billion was let for the construction, design, and development of one Advanced Technology Bomber prototype. A follow-on production run of 132 aircraft would follow with initial operational capability to take place in the early to mid-1990s.

The Advanced Technology Bomber specification dictated long range, high payload, and low observability. The specification as it was written all but spelled out the need for a flying-wing design.

By 1983 the shape and structure of the Advanced Technology Bomber was midway through the design process when the Air Force asked Northrop to explore a revised mission profile that would have the Advanced Technology Bombers operating in a low-altitude, terrain-following mode. The design that Northrop

The B-2A from its six o'clock position. The beavertail is angled slightly down and the flaps are in a lowered position. All four auxiliary inlet doors are open above the two inlets and the auxiliary power unit door is open to the left and lower edge of the left nacelle. At the rear of the main fuselage and just to the right of center is the standby air-speed device that was taken off once operational flight data was determined to be calibrated and reliable from the B-2A's own sensors. John Andrews collection

had been working on was optimized for high-altitude penetration. This new requirement led to a reassessment of the original design. After reviewing all the existing data, Northrop concluded that their flying-wing was still the best design, but many modifications would be necessary to make it an effective low-altitude penetration bomber. The Air Force ordered Northrop to make the changes, and the redesign resulted in the first flight being delayed about two years and added more than $1 billion in cost to the program.

The first B-2A liftoff and the first flight of a Northrop flying wing in almost forty years. Even at takeoff, the trailing edge drag flaps are in the partially open position. From this angle the wing looks lumpy when viewed down the leading edge of the wing from its nose to the outboard edge of the wing. John Andrews collection

As Northrop proceeded with the redesign, the Air Force declared the Advanced Technology Bomber program "black," placing it under the tightest of all security covers. With a program that was shielded from all but those with a need to know, the expenses of such a highly classified program became easy to mask or hide from those that normally oversee expensive government programs. It wasn't until the late 1980s that congress and the general public would see just how far over budget the Advanced Technology Bomber had gotten. Some would say it was all the fault of the prime contractors for the overrun, but as with most Department of Defense weapons program cost escalations, the biggest culprit was the ever-changing world we live in and the resulting change in mission requirements.

B-2A Production Go-Ahead

On 19 November 1987, with the design changes fully incorporated into the first aircraft and with production of the number one prototype well on its way, the Pentagon quietly appropriated $2 billion for the initial production of four Advanced Technology Bombers. With the formal production contract came the formal Air Force designation of B-2A.

The B-2A design as we see it today is an all flying wing design. More than eighty percent of the B-2A is built of composite materials, but conventional titanium and aluminum are used in the load-bearing structures.

The fuselage consists of a blended center-body accommodating the cockpit, two side-by-side bomb bays, as well as all

primary and secondary systems. All of the major assemblies converge in this area, which provides all the support carry through and accompanying bulkheads connections.

The cockpit consists of complete flight controls, instruments and displays for each of the two crew members and is fully pressurized and air conditioned. The cockpit is equipped with McDonnell Douglas ACES II upward-firing ejection seats. The cockpit is enclosed by four large low-observable wind screens. The crew reaches the cockpit by climbing a retractable ladder assembly mounted to the left and rear of the nose wheel assembly and enters through a hatch on the underside of the aircraft.

The cockpit controls are conventional in nature and consist of a single control stick and two rudder pedals for each crew member. One feature that makes the B-2A unique is the dual sets of throttle quadrants.

The instrument panel is an all "glass" type, where virtually all data is presented to the crew on full-color cathode ray tube screens in a T-style layout, three on the top and one centered underneath. Crew members have their own displays.

The entire aircraft, including the central fuselage area, is part of the wing area and contributes to total lift. The wing assembly is made up of composite materials impregnated with special

The first takeoff for a B-2A bomber at Air Force Plant 42, Palmdale, California. The crowd in the background is just in front of the EG&G company terminal that is used to ferry men and women back and forth from Palmdale to Groom Lake test facility in the Nevada desert. John Andrews collection

Next page
The Northrop B-2A flying wing takes on fuel from an Edwards-based NKC-135E. The NKC-135E is assigned to the Air Force System Command and is part of the B-2A Test Force located at Edwards. John Andrews collection

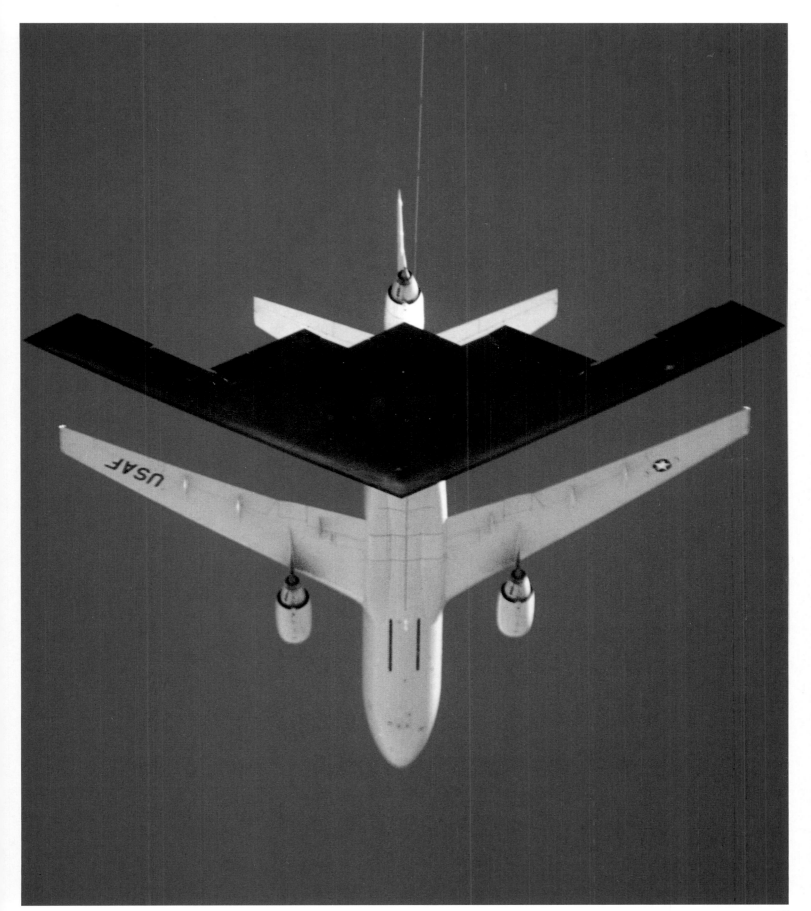

Previous page
A McDonnell Douglas KC-10A Extender and the number one B-2A perform air-to-air refueling over the Mojave Desert. Northrop

The B-2A's pilot has no way of knowing his position under the KC-10A or KC-135 other than to look at the light indicators mounted under the belly of the tanker. The rotating refueling receptacle of the B-2A can be clearly seen in this view. When not in use, the refueling receptacle rotates 180 degrees along the center axis of the aircraft. Northrop

epoxy resins. The wing assembly is made up of a single spar with a boxed carry through structure located in the center section of the fuselage/inboard wing assembly. The outer wing structure is built primarily of composite materials and attaches to the center section at the inboard spar and wing carry through box

assembly, which are made of high-strength titanium.

The leading edges of the B-2A are covered with a dielectric radar-absorbing material and is said to have a similar construction to that of the Lockheed SR-71 Blackbird. The leading edge sweep is at thirty-three degrees with the trailing

edge forming what is sometimes referred to as the "Double W" configuration. With the exception of the exhaust ejector assembly, virtually all the wings trailing edge consists of movable control surfaces.

The Northrop B-2A is equipped with a quad-redundant fly-by-wire system

An almost classic view of the first B-2A with its "Do Not Walk" areas clearly marked over the low-visibility paint on the top surface of the bomber. The serial number carried on all B-2As to date is located aft of the cockpit, midway, and centered on the main fuselage. Note the very dark leading edge, wing tips, and the extreme trailing edge points of the wing. Northrop

81

Previous page
The B-2A is extremely rigid when compared to conventional aircraft such as the B-52 or B-1B. Even so, very close examination of this photo will show that the outer left wing panel twists upward. To the rear of the wing, nearly all of the trailing edge consists of articulated control surfaces, except just aft of the engine exhaust ejectors Northrop

or B-83 freefall nuclear weapons. As configured for a conventional weapons load, the B-2A can carry up to eighty Mk. 62, Mk. 82, or Mk. 117 bombs, and other weapons yet to be identified.

B-2A Production Reduced

By 1990, the original Air Force requirement for 133 B-2As had been

As of this writing, the B-2A has been tested to just over 45,000 feet and a speed of 460 miles per hour. Also apparent in this photo is the severely recessed exhaust ejectors. This is required to reduce the B-2A's infrared signature. Northrop

reduced to seventy-five aircraft as a result of the 1991 deficit-reduction bill. The hopes of building a large fleet of B-2As came to an end with the announcement by President George Bush in the State of the Union address on 28 January 1992 that the administration would halt production at twenty aircraft. As the number of B-2As was cut, the unit cost rose enormously. The price tag rose from an original unit cost of $274 million in 1989 dollars to upwards of $1.5 billion because the B-2A's enormous research and development costs were now amortized over twenty units rather than 132. The B-2A is now the world's most expensive aircraft. By contrast, a *Nimitz* class nuclear-powered aircraft carrier, which carries a whole wing of fighters and attack aircraft and measures 1,150 feet by 420 feet, with a gross weight of over 90,000 tons, costs only as much as three B-2As.

The Air Force and Northrop have tried in vain to justify the B-2A's costs. The B-2A was designed to battle the now-crumbled Soviet Union. Even with the apparent success of the B-2A flight testing and only a few minor problems with low-observable testing, the decline of nuclear threats has made a large fleet of B-2As difficult to justify.

If the B-2A enters operational service, it will be assigned to Whiteman Air Force Base, Missouri, near the town of Knob Noster, and flown by the 509th Wing. Construction began in early 1988 to convert what had been a Minuteman II and Minuteman III missile base to support the B-2A. Aircraft last operated out of Whiteman in 1962. As of summer 1991, the Whiteman runways had been totally resurfaced, at least six new hangars had been constructed, and most of the wings support buildings had been completed.

All B-2A training will be handled out of Whiteman. Operations will be flown from Whiteman, with operational detachments possible at Diego Garcia in the Indian Ocean and Anderson Air Force Base, Guam. From these locations, a B-2A strike force could reach any target in the world with only one aerial refueling.

Only time will tell if the B-2A Stealth Bomber will follow the path of its flying-wing predecessors—to be relegated to flight test status only, or maybe sent directly from the production facility to the bone yard at Davis-Monthan Air Force Base, Arizona.

The number one B-2A on final approach to Edwards. The B-2A has gear down, drag brakes fully extended, and the beaver tail down about five degrees. The auxiliary inlet doors are also visible above and behind the primary inlets. John Andrews collection

The Lockheed YF-22 and Northrop YF-23 Advanced Tactical Fighters

In the summer of 1981 the Air Force issued a request for information about a stealthy air-superiority fighter to eventually replace the McDonnell Douglas F-15 Eagle. The new fighter would be called the Advance Tactical Fighter. The American aircraft industry responded with design concepts that ranged from a lightweight fighter tipping the scales at a little over 25,000 pounds (smaller than the F-16) to a Lockheed-designed aerial battle cruiser coming in at 120,000 pounds with a top speed of over Mach 3.

In the early 1980s the term "stealth" was not even in the conversations of most Advanced Tactical Fighter designers, with the exception of those from Lockheed, whose F-117A was flying out of the Groom Lake test facility, and Northrop, who had been actively working on the Advanced Tactical Bomber. Stealth technology had shown tremendous potential to counter radar-guided weapons and airborne- and ground-based radars. A 1981 Northrop paper defined a stealth fighter as one that could detect its opponent first and fire first, even if the hostile aircraft had a more powerful radar and a longer range missile.

The US Air Force's choice for their next air superiority fighter, the Lockheed YF-22. Lockheed

A man and his machine, chief Lockheed YF-22 test pilot Dave Ferguson poses with a YF-22. Lockheed

Along with stealth, the request for information specified that the aircraft be capable of "supercruise"—the ability to fly at supersonic speeds without the need to use the fuel-guzzling afterburners. Most fighters can fly at supersonic speeds for only a few minutes before their fuel is exhausted. A supercruise fighter can fly its entire mission at supersonic speeds without limiting its range. Responses to

Roll-out day for the first Lockheed YF-22A, built by the team of Lockheed, Boeing, and General Dynamics. This aircraft was powered by the General Electric F120-GE jet engine. The YF-22 did not carry an Air Force serial number, instead it carried a civil registration number of N22YF. The YF-22 was assembled and flown out of the Lockheed Plant 10 manufacturing production complex located at Air Force Plant 42, Palmdale, California. Lockheed

the request for information indicated that supercruise appeared to be practical and, because of the strides in engine performance over the last decade, affordable.

By late 1982, the Advanced Tactical Fighter began to gel into a system that made sense: It would have supercruise, a combat radius of up to 920 miles (an increase of almost sixty percent over the Air Force F-15A), and would be stealthy enough to elude other fighter aircrafts' radars.

Prime bidders were instructed to use the very best technology available with the knowledge that the program would not enter the production phase until 1992 or 1993, at the earliest. The hoped-for production totals would be 750 aircraft for the US Air Force, with an unknown additional quantity going to key allies— Britain's Royal Air Force and the Israeli Defense Force.

Formation of the Advanced Tactical Fighter Program Office

In 1983, the Air Force Advanced Tactical Fighter program office was formed at Wright-Patterson Air Force Base, Ohio, headed by Col. Albert C. Piccirillo. The task of the program office was to produce a specification that met all the Air Force's essential requirements.

After four complete drafts, the program office reached a near-final specification by the end of 1984. This specification called for the Advanced Tactical Fighter to have a combat radius of approximately 800 miles. This range would allow Advanced Tactical Fighters based in the United Kingdom to strike any target in Central Europe. The Advanced Tactical Fighter would be able to cruise at Mach 1.4 to 1.5 throughout the portion of a mission that required it to fly over enemy-occupied airspace (up to 300 miles in and out). Additional requirements spelled out a need to operate from airfields with less than 2,000 feet of usable runway at a gross weight of 50,000 pounds. All this for a flyaway cost of $40 million or less in 1985 dollars.

"Fly-Before-You-Buy"

In May 1986, Secretary of the Air Force Edward C. Aldridge announced

that the Air Force would order flying prototypes of two Advanced Tactical Fighter designs. One factor in making this decision was the "fly-before-you-buy" policy favored by the Packard Commission after a review of the Pentagon's procurement practices.

In the summer of 1986 the program experienced a consolidation when Lockheed, Boeing, and General Dynamics announced an agreement under which

Formation flying of the Lockheed team's two YF-22 Advanced Tactical Fighters. During the initial flight test segment of the fly-off, the two YF-22s logged 91.6 hours of flight time in seventy-four flights. The red apparatus on the back of the N22YF aircraft contains a spin recovery parachute required as a precaution for high-angle-of-attack testing. Prototype number two, N22YX, is powered by the winning Advanced Tactical Fighter engine, the Pratt & Whitney F119-PW. The Advanced Tactical Fighter engines are so powerful, that

to keep up with either YF-22, the F-16 chase planes were constantly going into full military power. The YF-22 proved its superior maneuverability during a series of test flights in December 1990. Operating at speeds as low as eighty knots and angles of attack as high as sixty degrees, the YF-22 demonstrated that it has no maneuverability restrictions and no angle-of-attack limits. The YF-22 is believed able to fly at angles of attack of ninety degrees at 1g. Lockheed

Future cockpit—advanced flight station technologies pictured in this artist's concept represent many being developed by Lockheed for integration into its F-22. Advancements include six flat panel color screens that allow for display of information on each screen, with the center three screens capable of forming one tactical panoramic view. An extra-wide head up display (HUD) provides flight and target information without diverting the pilot's attention from the surrounding airspace; similar information is contained on displays mounted in the pilot's helmet. The programmable nature of the displays eliminates the need for dedicated gauges and increases the amount of display space, necessary because of increased information coming in from the aircraft's more sophisticated sensors. A specially articulated pilot's seat automatically compensates for the increased and sustained gravitational forces the F-22 pilot will experience in flight. Lockheed/Eric Van Der Palen

they would team up to develop the Advanced Tactical Fighter if any of their proposals were selected for the fly off. A few weeks later, the team of Northrop and McDonnell Douglas announced a similar agreement. All that was left was for the Air Force to select a winner.

YF-22 and YF-23

The winners were announced in October 1986 in a statement made by Air

Force Secretary Aldridge; the winners, Lockheed and Northrop, would each build two flying prototypes for the Demonstration/Validation program. Lockheed's design would be designated YF-22, and Northrop's design would be designated YF-23. The Lockheed and Northrop designs were chosen because they both had experience in designing and building stealth aircraft.

Stealth was not a concept for Lockheed, it was a reality. While the requirements for the Advanced Tactical Fighter were being worked out, refined, and defined between 1981 and 1985, Lockheed had built, tested and flown the world's first true stealth aircraft, the F-117A. During the same time period, Northrop had completed most of an extensive risk-reduction program on the B-2A Advanced Technology Bomber, with most of the emphasis on the bomber's stealth characteristics. By 1985, both Lockheed and Northrop knew they could build a stealth fighter that would fly as well as any nonstealth fighter and that its fly-away cost would be about the same as for a new nonstealth fighter. To top it off, the Air Force believed they could do it too.

It came as no surprise that the first designs from both Lockheed and Northrop showed that stealth.

The calibration chamber at the Kelly Johnson Research and Development Center near Clarita, California. Employing a calibrated model mounted on a pylon, a Lockheed technician uses the chamber to verify the low radar signatures of antennas mounted on a YF-22 model. Lockheed

Next page
A YF-22 equipped with a special spin-recovery parachute apparatus performs a 360-degree roll during a series of test flights in December 1990. According to the test pilots, who called the YF-22's performance "unprecedented," the YF-22's unique thrust vectoring system doubled the aircraft's roll rate and increased the rate pilots can push the nose down by a factor of four. Lockheed

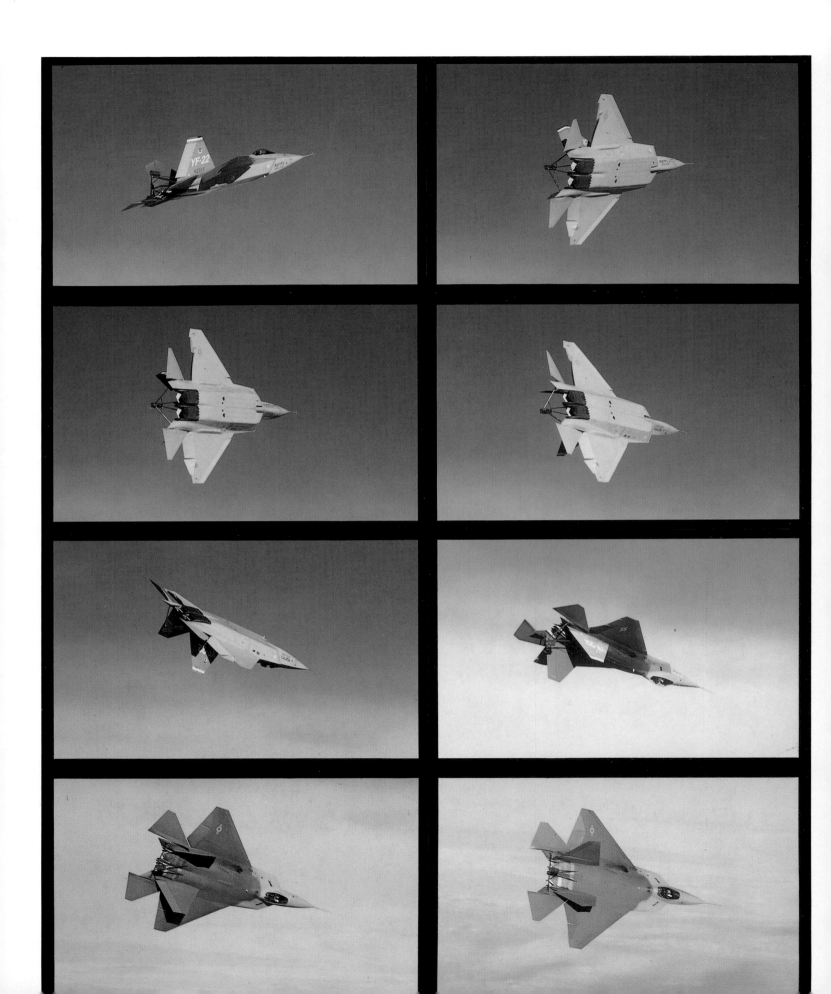

Previous page
The zig-zag edges around the exhaust
nozzles, the speed brakes, and other
apertures follow the same alignments—
parallel to the wing and tail leading edges.
Whatever radar energy may be reflected is
confined to a few aspects. Lockheed

The two-dimensional nozzles are heavier
and harder to cool than round nozzles but are
mechanically simpler and allow vectoring
and control of the exhaust plume shape. They
also permit a cleaner, more efficient after-
body or boat-tail design, particularly for a
twin-engine aircraft. Lockheed

(SSD), and the Prototype Air Vehicle
(PAV).

The Avionics Ground Prototype
section was a test bed for the entire suite
of sensors, transmitters, processors,
software, and displays. Both teams
choose to fly their Avionics Ground
Prototypes in airborne labs as a proof of
integration tool.

Under the Prototype Air Vehicle
section of the program, each team built
two flying prototypes: one powered by
the Pratt & Whitney F119-PW engine and
the other powered by the General
Electric F120-GE engine.

supercruise, and maneuverability could
be combined into one affordable aircraft.
In January 1986, the Air Force announced
that the deadlines for replies to the
Advanced Tactical Fighter request for
proposal would be extended to late April,
to give the other aerospace companies a

chance to work on their own stealth
design technologies.

The Demonstration/Validation was
outlined as a four-year program and was
divided into three major sections: the
Avionics Ground Prototype (AGP), the
Systems Specification Development

The YF-22s center fuselage was built by General Dynamics in Fort Worth, Texas. The wings were built by Boeing in Seattle, Washington. And the forward fuselage was built by the team leader, Lockheed's Advanced Development Projects Division, now called the Lockheed Advanced Development Company, or just plain Skunk Works.

The Skunk Works assembled the prototypes at Lockheed's Plant 10 production facility in Palmdale, California.

The two YF-23s were assembled by McDonnell Douglas at their assembly plant in St. Louis, Missouri, because the team leader, Northrop, was up to its ears in B-2A production work.

Both the YF-22 and YF-23 were built with working weapon bays for the purpose of testing weapon release concepts.

The Advanced Tactical Fighter prototypes were originally scheduled to fly in early 1990. But in early 1989,

Lockheed informed the Air Force that their entry would be late. The delay stemmed from a mid-1987 Lockheed decision to dramatically change the design of the YF-22 in order to reduce the weight. The Air Force agreed to extend the program by approximately six months.

YF-23 and YF-22 Roll-Outs

The Northrop YF-23 Prototype Air Vehicle One was rolled out at a media gathering at Edwards Air Force Base, California, on 22 June 1990, and made its first flight two months later, on 27 August 1990. This first YF-23 was powered by the Pratt & Whitney F-119-PW engine. YF-23 Prototype Air Vehicle Two first flew on 26 October 1990.

The Lockheed entry was unveiled on 29 August 1990 at the Lockheed Plant 10 production complex. The first YF-22 Prototype Air Vehicle made its maiden flight on 29 September 1990, from Palmdale to Edwards Air Force Base.

Six YF119-PW engines and three pitch-vectoring nozzles like those on the integrated unit shown in this photo have been fielded to support the current round of YF-22 flight testing at Edwards. This time-lapsed photo gives true meaning to vectored thrust. The initial flight production version of the YF119-PW will begin flight testing in the first eleven Full Scale Development (FSD) F-22A aircraft in mid-1995. Pratt & Whitney via Arnie Gunderson

The YF-22 number two prototype successfully launched an AIM-120 Advanced Medium-Range Air-To-Air Missile (AMRAAM) on 20 December 1990 during testing over the Pacific Missile Test Center near Point Mugu, California. Lockheed test pilot Tom Morgenfeld was at the controls. This launch, and an earlier launch of an AIM-9 Sidewinder by the same YF-22, marked the only weapons test during their combined Advanced Tactical Fighter flight-test program. Lockheed

Previous page
The wing of the YF-22 is almost a delta. The body above the inlets, aided by vortices shed from the nose chines, contributes significantly to the lift. Note how far forward the exhaust nozzles are. This is because the new engines are short in relationship to their thrust. Lockheed

Prominent in this view of the YF-22 are the large flaps, cut away at their roots to accommodate the stabilizer, and large vertical tails. Lockheed

YF-22 Prototype Air Vehicle Two first flew on 30 October 1990.

The supercruise milestones for the Advanced Tactical Fighter program were achieved in early November 1990. On 3 November, YF-22 Prototype Air Vehicle One (powered by General Electric F120 engine) became the first to surpass the

Air Force's supercruise benchmark, reaching Mach 1.58 on military power after less than twelve hours of flight testing. The Northrop YF-23 was not far behind reaching Mach 1.43 on 14 November.

The Advanced Tactical Fighter specification was more than enough to challenge the best engineers the aerospace community had to offer. Its requirements pulled the design of the airframe in opposing directions. At one point, two desired features led the team to the same design solution; a third solution, however, canceled out the first two.

YF-22 just after firing an AIM-120 missile from its lower weapons bay. If you look hard just under the aircraft inlet and in front of the wing leading edge, the doors are still in the launch position. Lockheed

Tom Morgenfeld, a Lockheed test pilot, flies the number two YF-22 over the Edwards test range. The size and overall visibility afforded by the bubble canopy are evident in this view. The ejection seat in the YF-22 and the production F-22A is the McDonnell Douglas ACES II, used in the F-15, F-16, F/A-18, B-2A, and the F-117A. It's a good seat that the Air Force highly believes in.
Lockheed

The required reduction in radar cross section was the most difficult part of the specification. The best way to reduce the Radar Cross Section of any aircraft is to look at all of its components or features and remove everything you possibly can that will cause a radar signal to bounce back. All one has to do is look at the B-2A and the canceled McDonnell Douglas-General Dynamics A-12. Neither of these aircraft have fins or

tail, but then again they were not designed to be agile and both are subsonic. By contrast, the Advanced Tactical Fighter was designed to fly supersonic and to be highly maneuverable, which required the fuselage to be long and slim with a large internal volume for fuel, the wings to be thin to reduce drag, and the tail surfaces large to provide agility.

As more and more information on the two competing prototypes became known, one common feature became apparent; both aircraft were about the same size—not surprising since both were designed for the same mission, to carry the same payload over the same range, and to use the same engines. It is also not surprising that the YF-22 and YF-23 are about the same size and weight as the F-15C they are designed to replace. The Advanced Tactical Fighter can hold sixty percent more fuel than the F-15C.

General Electric and Pratt & Whitney Engines

When the Air Force wrote the specification for the Advanced Tactical Fighter engines, state of the art advances suggested that the engines would have a thrust-to-weight ratio of 10:1.

Engine thrust is generally measured and rated at sea level at zero speed, while the engine is in maximum afterburner. The Advanced Tactical Fighter engines have a sea-level static thrust in full afterburner of approximately 35,000 pounds—which is the same amount of thrust generated by the world's only Mach 3-rated engine, the Pratt & Whitney J-58 that powers the SR-71. This figure is twenty percent greater than the newest versions of the F100-PW and the F110-GE that power the F-16C/D and the F-15C/D/E—and the Advanced Tactical Fighter engines derive a smaller portion of their total power from the use of the

afterburner than any of the other engines. At full military power (without afterburner) the Advanced Tactical Fighter engines produce more than thirty percent more power than the newest F110 or F100 and an astounding fifty-seven percent more power than the engine that powered the early F-15A/B. Furthermore, the Advanced Tactical Fighter engines have about the same thrust-to-weight ratio in military power as the F100 or F110 have in full afterburner. This advantage gives the Advanced Tactical Fighter between forty and sixty percent greater thrust-to-weight ratio throughout the flight envelope.

While the Advanced Tactical Fighter engines could be used in the F-15 or F-16, giving either aircraft the ability to fly in a supercruise mode, it is the aerodynamics of the Advanced Tactical Fighter airframes that give them their efficiency, range, and maneuverability.

Stealth

The Advanced Tactical Fighters' stealth design requirement created some of its own configuration considerations that were carried over in both the Lockheed and Northrop designs. With the need for supercruise and low observable features built into the same aircraft, all

A great shot of the second YF-22's right side taken in low light. The break in the surface of the YF-22's side shows off the AIM-9 weapons door in good detail. The overall size of the lower weapons bay shows up in this view as well. Lockheed

weapons would have to be carried internally, much like the Air Defense fighters of the early 1950s and 1960s.

Flying a stealth aircraft at supersonic speeds presented a problem with the typical supersonic inlet (variable inlet ramps, sharped-edged inlet openings and not-so-low-observable

The Arizona Air National Guard flew this KC-135E out of Sky Harbor Airport in Phoenix, Arizona. In chase is an F-16D from the Edwards Flight Test Center. The YF-22 is the second aircraft and is powered by the Pratt & Whitney F119-PW jet engine. Lockheed

by-pass doors); all these features that allow for efficient high speed flight are counter to all basic principle of low-observable design. The designs used on the B-2A, S-shaped inlet ducts or the gridded inlet of the F-117A would not work in a supersonic aircraft.

YF-22

In the YF-22, the inlets are fixed, having no movable ramps or doors. The inlet opening is angled in such a way as to reduce the radar cross section to a minimum. With the inboard lip well ahead of the outboard, the YF-22 inlet is of a "two-shock" design. At supercruise, the inner lip generates a shock wave that compresses the air and slows it down just before it reaches the outer lip. The outer

Next page
The mating and assembly fixture for the F-22 main wing assembly. The fixture can rotate 360 degrees on the X axis to allow technical personnel access to all aspects of the wing assembly without the need of scaffolding and walkways over and around the wing-assembly tool. Lockheed

lip creates its own shock wave, further slowing the airstream to subsonic speeds. This design recovers as much as ninety-five percent of the energy lost in the

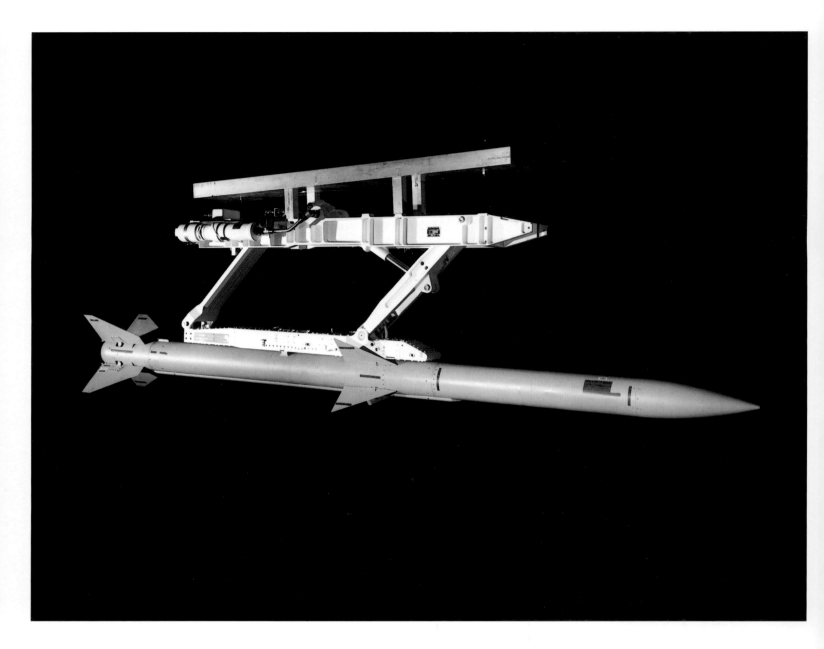

The first public released photo of the AMRAAM weapons pylon to be used on the F-22A production aircraft. The pylon extends the AIM-120 AMRAAM into the air flow for launch. The early Air Defense fighters such as the Convair F-109 and F-106 carried their weapons and launched them in the same manner. Lockheed

shock in the form of compression in the inlet duct, which in turn increases the power to the engine.

Most of the Lockheed YF-22's mass —the engines, inlets, weapons bays, landing gear, and most of the fuel load— is located in the box-like fuselage, which measures approximately thirty-eight by twenty feet. Most of the front end of the fuselage is taken up by the fixed inlet system, followed closely behind by the engine bays, which are located close together. The YF-22 has three weapons bays: one on each side of the inlet that can carry two short-range air-to-air missiles, such as the infrared-guided AIM-9R, and a longer centerline weapons bay with space for at least four AIM-120 radar-guided missiles. Closer observation will show that all three weapons bays are located aft of the inlets reducing the danger of the engines ingesting hot gas and propellant when the missiles are fired.

On the Lockheed-built YF-117's first flight, Lockheed's chief test pilot, Hal Farley, discovered that the all-moving tails of the early YF-117As were too small, and all production F-117As came off the assembly line with rudders fifty percent larger than those used on the YF-117. Farley said, "We didn't make that mistake again." The YF-22s verticals are seventy percent larger than the F-15s. They are not all-moving like the F-117A's, but they are fitted with large conventional rudders.

YF-23

At first glance, the Northrop YF-23 appears to be longer and sleeker than the Lockheed YF-22, while in reality, the two Advanced Tactical Fighters are nearly identical in size.

108

The overall view of the YF-23 at the time of roll-out was one of a forward fuselage and two engine nacelles hooked together by a diamond-shaped wing, followed up in the rear by two very large, outwardly angled, all-moving tails. The forward fuselage contains the cockpit, the nose landing gear assembly, the electronics bays, and the weapons bay, which can accommodate up to four AIM-120 missiles.

The design philosophy that gave the Northrop B-2A its smooth flowing contours is quite evident in the design of

the YF-23. All the surfaces are shaped into a series of compound curves of constantly changing radius. Under close observation, it appeared that the YF-23 was built using seamless construction techniques similar to those used on the B-2A.

When viewed from the top, the YF-23's wing forms a dramatic diamond shape. The leading edge of one wing and the trailing edge of the other wing are parallel. Like the YF-22, the YF-23's fuselage has a great deal of volume for fuel and the buried engines.

A Lockheed team YF-22 Advanced Tactical Fighter prototype flies in formation with F-15D and F-16D chase planes during flight testing at Edwards. Lockheed

While the YF-22's vertical tails appear to be too large, the YF-23's are even larger because they perform the pitch- and yaw-control of a conventional aircraft's vertical stabilizer/rudder and its horizontal stabilizers/elevators. To put the size of the YF-23's tail surfaces in perspective, each is as large as the entire

PROTOTYPE ACTIVE ARRAY RADAR SYSTEM

- **1000 T/R MODULES PRODUCED**
  - **MET DEM/VAL/COST/ PERFORMANCE TARGETS**
  - **DUAL PRODUCTION LINES**

- **ACTIVE VLO ARRAY**
  - **INTEGRATED WITH RADOME DESIGN**

- **INTEGRATED WITH CIP**

- **Ada SOFTWARE DEMONSTRATED**

UNCLASSIFIED

FSD.515 5-9-91

A view of the prototype Active Array Radar System that will be used on the F-22A. Lockheed

wing of the F/A-18 Hornet. The tails are canted fifty degrees outward from the vertical to reduce the chance of reflecting radar waves back to their source.

The YF-22 and the YF-23 were not designed to be the world's fastest fighter aircraft. Their designs are optimized for supercruise speeds of Mach 1.5 to 1.7. They can and will fly faster. Their top speeds are classified but are probably greater than Mach 2.

When it came time for the Air Force to pick the winner of the Advanced Tactical Fighter competition, it was able to choose between two excellent designs that were built to achieve the same goals, but under different design philosophies. Lockheed built an agile dogfighter's fighter that was stealthy. Northrop built and designed a stealth aircraft that flew like a fighter. Northrop's basic design was and is faster and more stealthy than the Lockheed design, and Lockheed will not argue the point. But in the end the Air Force decided that it valued agility more than stealth and speed, announcing in April 1991 that it had selected the Lockheed YF-22 as its air superiority fighter for the twenty-first century.

Roll-out day for the Northrop YF-23 at Edwards. This head-on view shows the large inlet bulges outboard on the bottom, the S style inlet ducts, the above-the-wing engine nacelles, and the fifty-degree outward angle of the twin rudders. James C. Goodall

This view shows the YF-23's enormous flaps, outboard ailerons, and leading edge slats. Just behind the nose-wheel gear assembly is the main weapons bay door in the open or launching position. Tony Landis

The only good view of the YF-23 cockpit to date, deliberately overexposed to bring out cockpit detail. From this angle it looks like a push-button airplane. Just in front of the pilot is a massive head up display and the canopy assembly's sawtooth trailing edge. Tony Landis

Air Force Flight Test Center test pilot, Maj. "Taco" Johnston prepares the number one YF-23 for a test flight from the Advanced Tactical Fighter compound at Edwards. John Andrews collection

The YF-23 with its main weapons bay open. Close observation will show the sawtooth wind deflectors on the lead edge of the bay. This reduces turbulence during weapons launch and offers a reduction in the radar cross section of the YF-23 at the time of missile launch. The dark green hose from the aircraft's right to the left wheel and tire assembly is used to cool the brakes after a short field landing and aborted take-off testing. John Andrews collection

The seamless stealth design philosophy developed for the B-2 has been adopted for the YF-23. Both aircraft have curvaceous lines in a head-on view. John Andrews collection

Just how big are the exhaust ejectors on the YF-23? Here's a good vantage point. Each engine nacelle is a separate feature on the YF-23, as can be seen from this angle. The bottom appears to be flat, acting as a lifting body during flight. **John Andrews collection**

In this view, flap size is evident. Despite the elimination of thrust reversers, the YF-23 was still designed to use less runway than the F-15 it was designed to replace. Northrop

*This view shows all the control surfaces in
deflected positions.* Northrop

The V tails are deflected at a dramatic angle to lift the YF-23's long nose off the ground at the lowest possible speeds, necessary because the YF-23 does not have vectored thrust. Northrop

The number one YF-23 takes off under full military power from its General Electric F120-GE engines. Northrop

The "Black Widow" markings on the YF-23 were put on for the photo calibration part of the flight-test program. It started out as just one triangle until some Northrop employee saw the historical significance of adding another triangle to the bottom, making the red hourglass of the black widow spider and harking back to the Northrop P-61 Black Widow night fighter of World War II. When Northrop management saw this view and the name that went with it, they ordered the hourglass removed and all released photos showing this configuration destroyed. They forbade anyone from using the name "black widow" for any reason. John Andrews collection

The two YF-23s fly in formation over the Edwards Test Range. The YF-23s flew with two different paint schemes—number one carried a dark gunship gray paint job, while number two flew with a light-gray two-tone pattern, similar to the F-15's pattern. Northrop

A rare view of three of the four Advanced Tactical Fighter candidates in the air at the same time. Just to the rear of the lead YF-23 is the winning candidate, the YF-22. This photo was taken from the boomers position of a KC-135 tanker over the Mojave Desert. James C. Goodall collection

Previous page
Northrop went to great lengths to reduce the number of edges on the YF-23. The lines of the unique rhomboidal wing are followed in the massive V tails. The YF-23's wing meets the body only a few feet aft of the canopy, eliminating the need for leading-edge root extensions. The downward view from the cockpit is excellent. Northrop

A KC-135A, serial number 56-3651, from Fairchild Air Force Base, Washington, refuels YF-23 number one as an Air Force Flight Test Center F-15 flies chase. The three aircraft are from three distinctly different eras; the KC-135A was built in 1956, the F-15A was manufactured in 1976, and the YF-23 designed in 1987 and first flown in 1990. Northrop

The first YF-23 on final approach to the Edwards runway. The pilot sits high up in the YF-23's cockpit, giving him excellent visibility in all directions. Northrop

The YF-23 banks over the Edwards Air Force Base golf course and housing area during a photo session. Visible are the lead edge extensions in a ten-degrees-down position, the all-moving tail assembly canted just a bit in the turn, and a prominent emblem just behind the inlet is the Pratt & Whitney Dependable Eagle badge. Northrop

Paul Metz, chief test pilot for the YF-23 program, joined Northrop in 1980 as a flight and control engineer and was subsequently named as an engineering test pilot. In 1985, Metz was named chief test pilot for the Aircraft Division of Northrop. Metz has more than 5,000 hours of flying experience in over sixty types of aircraft, including F-105, F-4, A-37, F-86, F-5, F-15, F-20, and YF-23. Northrop

The second YF-23 prepares to refuel from a KC-135 tanker. The refueling door is open midway back on top of the fuselage just above the Air Force System Command emblem. The blending curves show up well in this view of the YF-23. Northrop

The hopes and dreams of the Northrop Corporation for the twenty-first century, in a family portrait at Edwards Air Force Base. With the B-2A production ending at twenty airframes, and the loss of the Advanced Tactical Fighter contract to the team of Lockheed, Boeing, and General Dynamics, Northrop's future as an aircraft builder seems in doubt. Northrop

Index